one pots

100 EASY RECIPES
one pots

bay books

contents

chicken and duck

chicken and coconut milk soup

150 g (5½ oz) dried rice vermicelli
1 lime
4 small red chillies, seeded and chopped
1 onion, chopped
2 garlic cloves, crushed
4 thin slices fresh ginger, finely chopped
2 lemongrass stems (white part only), chopped
1 tablespoon chopped coriander (cilantro) leaves
1 tablespoon peanut oil
750 ml (26 fl oz/3 cups) chicken stock
685 ml (23½ fl oz/2¾ cups) coconut milk
500 g (1 lb 2 oz) chicken tenderloins, cut into thin strips
4 spring onions (scallions), chopped
150 g (5½ oz) fried tofu puffs, sliced
90 g (3 oz/1 cup) bean sprouts
3 teaspoons soft brown sugar

serves 8

method Soak the vermicelli in boiling water for 5 minutes. Drain, cut into short lengths. Remove the lime zest with a vegetable peeler and cut it into long, thin strips.

Place the chilli, onion, garlic, ginger, lemongrass and coriander into a food processor and process in short bursts for 20 seconds, or until smooth.

Heat the oil in a large heavy-based saucepan over medium heat. Add the chilli mixture and cook, stirring frequently, for 3 minutes, or until fragrant. Add the stock, coconut milk and lime zest strips, and bring to the boil. Add the chicken and cook, stirring, for 4 minutes, or until tender.

Add the spring onion, tofu, bean sprouts and brown sugar, and season with salt. Stir over medium heat for 3 minutes, or until the spring onion is tender. Divide the noodles among eight bowls and pour the soup over the top. Garnish with chilli and coriander.

100 EASY RECIPES ONE-POTS

avgolemono with chicken

1 onion, halved
2 cloves
1 carrot, cut into chunks
1 bay leaf
500 g (1 lb 2 oz) boneless, skinless
chicken breasts
75 g (2½ oz/⅓ cup) short-grain rice
3 eggs, separated
60 ml (2 fl oz/¼ cup) lemon juice
2 tablespoons chopped flat-leaf
(Italian) parsley
4 thin lemon slices, to garnish

serves 4

method Stud the onion halves with the cloves and then place in a large saucepan with 1.5 litres (52 fl oz/6 cups) water. Add the carrot, bay leaf and chicken. Season with salt and freshly ground black pepper. Slowly bring to the boil, reduce the heat and simmer for 10 minutes, or until chicken is cooked.

Strain the stock into a clean saucepan, reserving the chicken and discarding the vegetables. Add the rice to the stock, bring to the boil, then reduce the heat and simmer for 15 minutes, or until tender. Tear the chicken into shreds.

Whisk the egg whites until stiff peaks form, then beat in the yolks. Slowly beat in the lemon juice. Gently stir in 150 ml (5 fl oz) of the hot (not boiling) soup and beat thoroughly. Add the egg mixture to the soup and stir gently over low heat until thickened slightly. It should still be quite thin. Do not let it boil or the eggs may scramble. Add the shredded chicken, and season to taste.

Set aside for 3–4 minutes to allow the flavours to develop, then sprinkle with the parsley. Garnish with lemon slices and serve.

mulligatawny

30 g (1 oz) butter
375 g (13 oz) chicken thigh cutlets, skin and
 fat removed
1 large onion, finely chopped
1 apple, peeled, cored and diced
1 tablespoon curry paste
2 tablespoons plain (all-purpose) flour
750 ml (26 fl oz/3 cups) chicken stock
50 g (2 oz/¼ cup) basmati rice
1 tablespoon chutney
1 tablespoon lemon juice
60 ml (2 fl oz/¼ cup) cream

serves 4

method Gently heat the butter in a large heavy-based saucepan. Cook the chicken on medium–high heat for 5 minutes, or until browned, then remove and set aside. Add the onion, apple and curry paste to the pan. Cook for 5 minutes, or until the onion is soft. Stir in the flour and cook for 2 minutes, then add half the stock. Continue stirring until the mixture boils and thickens.

Return the chicken to the pan with the remaining stock. Stir until boiling, then reduce the heat, cover and simmer for 1 hour. Add the rice for the last 15 minutes of cooking.

Remove the chicken from the pan. Remove the meat from the bones, shred and return to the pan. Add the chutney, lemon juice and cream, and season to taste.

100 EASY RECIPES ONE-POTS

roast duck and noodle broth

3 dried shiitake mushrooms
1 Chinese roast duck (1.5 kg/3 lb 5 oz)
500 ml (17 fl oz/2 cups) chicken stock
2 tablespoons light soy sauce
1 tablespoon Chinese rice wine
2 teaspoons sugar
400 g (14 oz) fresh flat rice noodles
2 tablespoons oil
3 spring onions (scallions), thinly sliced
1 teaspoon finely chopped fresh ginger
400 g (14 oz) bok choy (pak choy), leaves separated
¼ teaspoon sesame oil

serves 4–6

method Soak the mushrooms in 250 ml (9 fl oz/1 cup) boiling water for 20 minutes. Drain, reserving the liquid and squeezing the excess liquid from the mushrooms. Discard the stems and thinly slice the caps.

Remove the skin and flesh from the duck. Discard the fat and carcass. Finely slice the duck meat and the skin (you need about 400 g/14 oz of duck meat).

Place the stock, soy sauce, rice wine, sugar and the reserved mushroom liquid in a saucepan over medium heat. Bring to a simmer and cook for 5 minutes.

Meanwhile, place the rice noodles in a heatproof bowl, cover with boiling water and soak briefly. Gently separate the noodles with your hands and drain well. Divide evenly among large soup bowls.

Heat the oil in a wok over high heat. Add the spring onion, ginger and mushroom, and cook for several seconds. Transfer to the broth with the bok choy and duck meat, and simmer for 1 minute, or until the duck has warmed through and the bok choy has wilted. Ladle the soup on the noodles and drizzle sesame oil on each serving. Serve immediately.

chicken marsala

60 ml (2 fl oz/¼ cup) olive oil
3 leeks (white part only), thinly sliced
1 teaspoon finely chopped rosemary
3 bay leaves, torn
1 kg (2 lb 4 oz) chicken pieces
seasoned plain (all-purpose) flour
1 large eggplant (aubergine), cut into cubes
2 zucchini (courgettes), roughly chopped
125 ml (4 fl oz/½ cup) Marsala (see Note)
300 ml (10½ fl oz) chicken stock
500 g (1 lb 2 oz/2 cups) tomato paste
    (concentrated purée)
200 g (7 oz) button mushrooms, halved

serves 4

method Heat the oil in a large heavy-based saucepan. Fry the leek, rosemary and bay leaves over low heat for 5 minutes, or until soft, stirring occasionally. Remove with a slotted spoon, leaving as much oil in the pan as possible.

Toss the chicken pieces in the seasoned flour. Add the chicken to the pan and brown well in batches over medium heat. Return all the chicken to the pan with the leek mixture.

Add the eggplant and zucchini, and cook, stirring, for 2–3 minutes, or until softened, turning the chicken over. Add the Marsala and stock, and cook for 15 minutes over medium–high heat.

Add the tomato paste and season well with salt and pepper. Bring to the boil, turning the chicken pieces in the sauce. Reduce the heat to a very gentle simmer, then cover and cook for 35 minutes. Add the mushrooms and cook, uncovered, for 5 minutes.

note *Marsala is a famous Italian fortified wine. It has a smoky, rich flavour and ranges from dry to sweet.*

chicken and cider stew with mash

1 kg (2 lb 4 oz) skinless, boneless chicken
thighs, cut into 2 cm (3/4 inch) cubes
1½ tablespoons finely chopped thyme
1 tablespoon oil
90 g (3 oz) butter
3 French shallots (eschalots), thinly sliced
375 ml (13 fl oz/1½ cups) apple cider
1 kg (2 lb 4 oz) potatoes, cubed
2 large green apples, peeled, cored and sliced
into eighths
170 ml (5½ fl oz/⅔ cup) cream
thyme sprigs, to garnish

serves 4

method Season the chicken thighs with 2 teaspoons of the thyme and salt and black pepper. Heat the oil and 20 g (3/4 oz) of the butter in a large saucepan over medium–high heat. Cook the chicken in two batches for 2–3 minutes, or until evenly browned. Remove from the pan.

Add the shallots and the remaining thyme to the pan, and sauté for 2 minutes. Pour in the cider, then bring to the boil, scraping off any sediment that has stuck to the bottom of the pan. Return the chicken to the pan and cover. Reduce the heat to low–medium and cook for 35–40 minutes, or until the chicken is tender and the sauce has reduced (check every now and then to see if any water needs to be added to the sauce).

Meanwhile, cook the potato and apple in a saucepan of boiling water for 15–20 minutes, or until tender. Drain and return to the pan over low heat for 1 minute to allow any water to evaporate. Remove from the heat, and mash with a potato masher. With a wooden spoon, stir in 2 tablespoons of the cream and the remaining butter, then season to taste with salt and pepper.

Gently stir the remaining cream into the chicken stew and cook for a further 2–4 minutes, or until the sauce has thickened. Garnish with thyme sprigs and serve at once with the potato and apple mash and a crisp green salad.

chinese braised chicken

250 ml (9 fl oz/1 cup) soy sauce
1 cinnamon stick
90 g (3 oz/⅓ cup) sugar
80 ml (2½ fl oz/⅓ cup) balsamic vinegar
2.5 cm (1 inch) piece fresh ginger, thinly sliced
4 garlic cloves
¼ teaspoon dried chilli flakes
1.5 kg (3 lb 5 oz) chicken pieces (skin removed)
1 tablespoon sesame seeds, toasted

serves 4–6

method Combine 1 litre (35 fl oz/4 cups) water with the soy sauce, cinnamon stick, sugar, balsamic vinegar, ginger, garlic and chilli flakes in a saucepan. Bring to the boil, then reduce the heat and simmer for 5 minutes.

Add the chicken pieces and simmer, covered, for 50 minutes, or until cooked through. Serve the chicken on a bed of steamed vegetables, drizzled with the poaching liquid and sprinkled with toasted sesame seeds.

100 EASY RECIPES ONE-POTS

chicken and mushroom casserole

20 g (¾ oz) dried porcini mushrooms
1.5 kg (3 lb 5 oz) chicken pieces
30 g (1 oz/¼ cup) seasoned plain (all-purpose)
flour
2 tablespoons oil
1 large onion, chopped
2 garlic cloves, crushed
60 ml (2 fl oz/¼ cup) chicken stock
80 ml (2½ fl oz/⅓ cup) white wine
400 g (14 oz) tin whole peeled tomatoes
1 tablespoon balsamic vinegar
3 thyme sprigs
1 bay leaf
300 g (10½ oz) field mushrooms, thickly sliced
thyme leaves, extra, to garnish

serves 4

method Lightly toss the chicken in the seasoned flour to coat, and shake off any excess.

Heat the oil in a flameproof casserole dish, and cook the chicken over medium heat in batches until well browned all over. Set aside. Add the onion and garlic to the casserole dish, and cook for 3–5 minutes, or until the onion softens. Stir in the chicken stock.

Return the chicken to the dish with the porcini mushrooms (and any remaining liquid), wine, tomatoes, vinegar, thyme sprigs and bay leaf. Cover and bake for 30 minutes.

After 30 minutes, remove the lid and add the field mushrooms. Return to the oven and cook, uncovered, for 15–20 minutes, or until the sauce thickens slightly. Garnish with thyme leaves and serve with a salad.

thai duck and pineapple curry

1 tablespoon peanut oil
8 spring onions (scallions), sliced on the
diagonal into 3 cm (1¼ inch) lengths
2 garlic cloves, crushed
2–4 tablespoons Thai red curry paste
750 g (1 lb 10 oz) Chinese roast duck, chopped
400 ml (14 fl oz) tin coconut milk
450 g (1 lb) tin pineapple pieces in syrup,
drained
3 makrut (kaffir lime) leaves
1 large handful coriander (cilantro) leaves,
chopped, plus extra leaves, to garnish
2 tablespoons chopped mint, plus extra leaves,
to garnish

serves 4–6

method Heat a wok until very hot, add the peanut oil and swirl to coat the side. Add the spring onion, garlic and red curry paste, and stir-fry for 1 minute, or until fragrant.

Add the roast duck, coconut milk, pineapple pieces, makrut leaves, and half each of the coriander and mint. Bring to the boil, then reduce the heat and simmer for 10 minutes, or until the duck is heated through and the sauce has thickened slightly. Stir in the remaining fresh herbs. Garnish with extra coriander and mint leaves and serve with steamed jasmine rice.

vietnamese chicken curry

4 large chicken leg quarters (leg and thigh
pieces)
1 tablespoon general-purpose Indian
curry powder
1 teaspoon caster (superfine) sugar
80 ml (2½ fl oz/⅓ cup) oil
500 g (1 lb 2 oz) orange sweet potato, cut into
3 cm (1¼ inch) cubes
1 large onion, cut into thin wedges
4 garlic cloves, chopped
1 lemongrass stem (white part only), finely
chopped
2 bay leaves
1 large carrot, cut into 1 cm (½ inch) pieces on
the diagonal
400 ml (14 fl oz) tin coconut milk

serves 6

method Remove the skin and any excess fat from the chicken. Pat dry with paper towels and cut each piece into 3 even pieces, making 12 pieces. Place the curry powder, sugar, ½ teaspoon black pepper and 2 teaspoons salt in a bowl, and mix well. Rub the curry mixture into the chicken pieces. Place the chicken on a plate, cover with plastic wrap and put in the refrigerator overnight.

Heat the oil in a large saucepan. Add the sweet potato and cook over medium heat for 3 minutes, or until lightly golden. Remove with a slotted spoon.

Remove all but 2 tablespoons of the oil from the pan. Add the onion and cook, stirring, for 5 minutes. Then add the garlic, lemongrass and bay leaves, and cook for 2 minutes.

Add the chicken and cook, stirring, over medium heat for 5 minutes, or until the chicken is well coated in the mixture and starting to change colour. Add 250 ml (9 fl oz/1 cup) water and simmer, covered, for 20 minutes. Stir once or twice.

Stir in the carrot, sweet potato and coconut milk, and simmer on a low heat, uncovered, stirring occasionally, for 30 minutes, or until the chicken is cooked and tender. Be careful not to break up the sweet potato cubes. Serve with steamed rice or rice stick noodles.

chicken with feta and olives

2 tablespoons oil
8 chicken pieces (1.2 kg/2 lb 10 oz)
1 onion, chopped
25 g (1 oz) oregano, leaves picked
2 tablespoons tomato paste (concentrated purée)
2 x 400 g (14 oz) tins chopped tomatoes
150 g (5½ oz) black olives
150 g (5½ oz) feta, crumbled, to serve

serves 4

method Heat half the oil in a saucepan and cook the chicken pieces, in batches, for 3–4 minutes, or until golden. Remove from the pan and set aside.

In the same saucepan, heat the remaining oil and cook the onion and half the oregano leaves for 3 minutes, or until the onion is softened. Add the tomato paste to the onion mixture and stir for 2 minutes, then add the tomato and the chicken pieces.

Simmer, covered, for 40–50 minutes, or until the chicken is cooked through. Add the olives and remaining oregano leaves. To serve, spoon into bowls and top with the crumbled feta.

100 EASY RECIPES ONE-POTS

balti chicken

1 kg (2 lb 4 oz) chicken thigh fillets
80 ml (2½ fl oz/⅓ cup) oil
1 large red onion, finely chopped
4–5 garlic cloves, finely chopped
1 tablespoon grated fresh ginger
2 teaspoons ground cumin
2 teaspoons ground coriander
1 teaspoon ground turmeric
½ teaspoon chilli powder
425 g (15 oz) tin chopped tomatoes
1 green capsicum (pepper), cut into 3 cm
(1¼ inch) cubes
1–2 small green chillies, seeded and finely
chopped
1 very large handful chopped coriander
(cilantro) leaves
2 spring onions (scallions), chopped to garnish

serves 6

method   Remove any excess fat or sinew from the chicken thigh fillets and cut into 4–5 pieces.

Heat a large wok over high heat, add the oil and swirl to coat the side. Add the onion and stir-fry over medium heat for 5 minutes, or until softened but not browned. Add the garlic and ginger, and stir-fry for 3 minutes.

Add the spices, 1 teaspoon salt and 60 ml (2 fl oz/¼ cup) water. Increase heat to high and stir-fry for 2 minutes, or until mixture thickens.

Add the tomato and 250 ml (9 fl oz/1 cup) water and cook, stirring often, for a further 10 minutes, or until the mixture is thick and pulpy and the oil comes to the surface.

Add the chicken to the wok, reduce the heat and simmer, stirring often, for 15 minutes. Add the capsicum and chilli, and simmer for 25 minutes, or until the chicken is tender. Add a little water if the mixture is too thick. Stir in the coriander and garnish with the spring onion. Serve with rice.

madrid chicken

1 orange
1 tablespoon olive oil
4 chicken breasts (skin and excess fat
   removed)
2 chorizo sausages (about 200 g/7 oz), cut into
   1 cm (½ inch) slices (see Note)
250 ml (9 fl oz/1 cup) chicken stock
250 g (9 oz/1 cup) bottled tomato pasta sauce
12 kalamata olives
kalamata olives, extra, to garnish
flat-leaf (Italian) parsley, to garnish

serves 4

method Using a vegetable peeler, carefully cut 4 thin strips of orange zest (about 1 x 4 cm/½ x 1½ inches). Remove the peel and pith from the orange, and segment the flesh.

Heat the oil in a saucepan and brown the chicken and chorizo slices, in batches if necessary. (Leave the meat side of the chicken browning for 5 minutes.) Add the stock, tomato sauce and orange zest. Bring to the boil, then reduce the heat and simmer, covered, for 25 minutes.

Remove the lid, turn the chicken over and continue to simmer, uncovered, for about 25 minutes, or until the chicken is tender and the sauce reduced. Season with salt and freshly ground black pepper, and stir through the olives and orange segments. Garnish with extra olives and flat-leaf parsley.

note *Chorizo sausages can be replaced with any spicy sausages.*

lemon and rosemary chicken stew

8 large chicken drumsticks
60 g (2 oz) butter
2 garlic cloves, crushed
2 teaspoons finely grated lemon zest
2 tablespoons chopped rosemary
1 tablespoon plain (all-purpose) flour
375 ml (13 fl oz/1 ½ cups) chicken stock
2 tablespoons lemon juice

serves 4

method Using a sharp knife, make two deep cuts in the thickest part of each chicken drumstick.

Melt the butter in a large frying pan. Add the drumsticks and cook over medium heat for 2 minutes on each side, or until brown. Add the garlic, lemon zest and rosemary.

Blend the flour, stock and lemon juice until smooth. Add to the pan and bring to the boil. Reduce the heat and simmer, covered, for 25 minutes, or until the drumsticks are tender, stirring occasionally. Season, and serve, ladling the sauce over the chicken. Delicious with green beans.

hint *To check whether chicken is cooked, insert a skewer into the thickest part. If the juice runs clear, the chicken is cooked.*

chicken kapitan

1 teaspoon small dried shrimp
80 ml (2½ fl oz/⅓ cup) oil
6–8 red chillies, seeded and finely chopped
4 garlic cloves, finely chopped
3 lemongrass stems (white part only),
  finely chopped
2 teaspoons ground turmeric
10 macadamia nuts
2 large onions, chopped
250 ml (9 fl oz/1 cup) coconut milk
1.5 kg (3 lb 5 oz) chicken, cut into 8 pieces
125 ml (4 fl oz/½ cup) coconut cream
2 tablespoons lime juice
lime wedges, to serve

serves 4–6

method Put the shrimp in a frying pan and dry-fry (no oil) over a low heat, shaking the pan regularly, for 3 minutes, or until the shrimp are dark orange and are giving off a strong aroma. Transfer to a mortar and pound with a pestle until finely ground. Alternatively, you may process in a food processor.

Place half of the oil, the chilli, garlic, lemongrass, turmeric and nuts in a food processor, and process in short bursts until very finely chopped, regularly scraping down the side of the bowl.

Heat the remaining oil in a wok or frying pan, add the onion and ¼ teaspoon salt, and cook, stirring regularly, over low heat for 8 minutes, or until golden.

Add the spice mixture and ground shrimp, and stir for 5 minutes. If the mixture begins to stick, add 2 tablespoons of the coconut milk. It is important to cook the mixture thoroughly to allow the flavours to develop.

Add the chicken to the wok and cook, stirring, for 5 minutes, or until beginning to brown. Stir in the remaining coconut milk and 250 ml (9 fl oz/1 cup) water, and bring to the boil. Reduce the heat and simmer for 50 minutes, or until the chicken is cooked and the sauce has thickened slightly. Add the coconut cream and bring the mixture back to the boil, stirring constantly. Add the lime juice and serve immediately with rice and lime wedges.

100 EASY RECIPES ONE-POTS

chilli chicken with tacos

1 tablespoon olive oil
1 onion, finely chopped
500 g (1 lb 2 oz) minced (ground) chicken
1–2 teaspoons mild chilli powder
440 g (15½ oz) tin chopped tomatoes
2 tablespoons tomato paste (concentrated purée)
1–2 teaspoons soft brown sugar
425 g (15 oz) tin red kidney beans, drained and rinsed
taco shells, or corn chips, to serve
sour cream, to serve

serves 4

method Heat the oil in a large saucepan. Add the chopped onion and cook over medium heat for 3 minutes, or until soft. Increase the heat to high and add the chicken. Cook until the chicken has browned, breaking up any lumps with a wooden spoon.

Add the chilli powder to the chicken and cook for 1 minute. Stir in the tomato, tomato paste and 125 ml (4 fl oz/½ cup) water.

Bring to the boil, then reduce the heat and simmer for 30 minutes. Stir through the sugar to taste and the kidney beans. Season. Serve along with warmed corn chips or in taco shells with the sour cream.

nonya chicken curry

curry paste

2 red onions, chopped
4 small red chillies, seeded and sliced
4 garlic cloves, sliced
2 lemongrass stems (white part only), sliced
3 cm x 2 cm (1¼ inch x ¾ inch) piece fresh
   galangal, sliced
8 makrut (kaffir lime) leaves, roughly chopped
1 teaspoon ground turmeric
½ teaspoon shrimp paste, roasted (see Note)

2 tablespoons oil
750 g (1 lb 10 oz) chicken thigh fillets, cut into
   bite-sized pieces
400 ml (14 fl oz) tin coconut milk
60 g (2 oz/¼ cup) tamarind purée
1 tablespoon fish sauce
3 makrut (kaffir lime) leaves, finely shredded,
   to garnish

serves 4

method To make the curry paste, place all the ingredients in a food processor or blender and process to a thick paste.

Heat a wok or large saucepan over high heat, add the oil and swirl to coat the side. Add the curry paste and cook, stirring occasionally, over low heat for 8–10 minutes, or until fragrant. Add the chicken and stir-fry with the paste for 2–3 minutes.

Add the coconut milk, tamarind purée and fish sauce to the wok, and simmer, stirring occasionally, for 15–20 minutes, or until the chicken is tender. Garnish with the makrut leaves. Serve with rice and steamed bok choy (pak choy).

note *To dry-roast the shrimp paste, wrap it in foil and place it under a hot grill (broiler) for 1 minute.*

100 EASY RECIPES ONE-POTS

chicken curry with apricots

18 dried apricots
1 tablespoon ghee or oil
2 x 1.5 kg (3 lb 5 oz) chickens, cut into pieces
3 onions, thinly sliced
1 teaspoon grated fresh ginger
3 garlic cloves, crushed
3 large green chillies, seeded and finely chopped
1 teaspoon cumin seeds
1 teaspoon chilli powder
½ teaspoon ground turmeric
4 cardamom pods, bruised
4 large tomatoes, peeled and cut into eighths (see Note)

serves 6–8

method Soak the dried apricots in 250 ml (9 fl oz/1 cup) hot water for 1 hour.

Melt the ghee in a large saucepan, add the chicken in batches and cook over high heat for 5–6 minutes, or until browned. Remove from the pan. Add the onion and cook, stirring often, for 10 minutes, or until the onion has softened and turned golden brown.

Add the ginger, garlic and chopped chilli, and cook, stirring, for 2 minutes. Stir in the cumin seeds, chilli powder and ground turmeric, and cook for a further 1 minute.

Return the chicken to the pan, add the cardamom, tomato and apricots, with any remaining liquid, and mix well. Simmer, covered, for 35 minutes, or until the chicken is tender.

Remove the chicken, cover and keep warm. Bring the liquid to the boil and boil rapidly, uncovered, for 5 minutes, or until it has thickened slightly. To serve, spoon the liquid over the chicken. Serve with steamed rice mixed with raisins, grated carrot and toasted flaked almonds.

note *To peel the tomatoes, score a cross in the base of each one, then cover with boiling water for 30 seconds. Drain, then cool under cold water. Peel the skin away from the cross.*

chicken with balsamic vinegar

2 tablespoons olive oil
8 chicken pieces
125 ml (4 fl oz/½ cup) chicken stock
125 ml (4 fl oz/½ cup) dry white wine
125 ml (4 fl oz/½ cup) balsamic vinegar
  (see Note)
40 g (1½ oz) chilled butter

serves 4

method Heat the oil in a large flameproof casserole dish over medium heat and cook the chicken, in batches, for 7–8 minutes, or until browned. Pour off any excess fat.

Add the stock, bring to the boil, then reduce the heat and simmer, covered, for 30 minutes, or until the chicken is cooked through.

Add the white wine and vinegar and increase the heat to high. Boil for 1 minute, or until the liquid has thickened. Remove from the heat, stir in the butter until melted, and season. Spoon the sauce over the chicken to serve, accompanied by roast potatoes and salad.

note *Use a good-quality balsamic vinegar, as the cheaper varieties can be too acidic.*

100 EASY RECIPES ONE-POTS

moroccan chicken

1 tablespoon Moroccan spice blend (see Note)
800 g (1 lb 12 oz) skinless, boneless chicken
thighs, halved
1 tablespoon oil
60 g (2 oz) butter
1 large onion, cut into wedges
1 cinnamon stick
2 garlic cloves, crushed
2 tablespoons lemon juice
250 ml (9 fl oz/1 cup) chicken stock
75 g (2½ oz/⅓ cup) pitted prunes, halved
280 g (10 oz/1½ cups) couscous
lemon wedges, to serve

serves 4

method Sprinkle half the spice blend over the chicken. Heat the oil and 20 g (¾ oz) of the butter in a large deep-sided frying pan over medium heat. Cook the chicken in batches for 5 minutes, or until evenly browned. Remove from the pan, then add the onion and cinnamon stick, and cook for 2–3 minutes before adding the garlic. Return the chicken to the pan and add the lemon juice and the remaining spice blend. Season to taste with salt and pepper, then cook, covered, for 5 minutes.

Add the stock and prunes to the pan, and bring to the boil. Reduce the heat to low–medium and cook, uncovered, for 15 minutes, or until the chicken is cooked and the liquid has reduced. Before serving, stir 20 g (¾ oz) of the butter into the sauce.

About 10 minutes before the chicken is ready, place the couscous in a heatproof bowl, add 375 ml (13 fl oz/1½ cups) boiling water and stand for 3–5 minutes. Stir in the remaining butter and fluff the couscous with a fork until the butter has melted and the grains have separated. Serve with the chicken and lemon wedges.

note *Depending on the quality and freshness of the Moroccan spice blend you buy, you may need to use a little more than specified in the recipe.*

duck and coconut curry

curry paste

1 red onion, chopped
2 garlic cloves
2 coriander (cilantro) roots, chopped
2 teaspoons chopped fresh ginger
1½ teaspoons coriander seeds, dry-roasted
   and ground
1 teaspoon cardamom seeds, dry-roasted
   and ground
1 teaspoon fenugreek seeds, dry-roasted
   and ground
1 teaspoon brown mustard seeds, dry-roasted
   and ground
10 black peppercorns, ground
2 teaspoons garam masala
¼ teaspoon ground turmeric
2 teaspoons tamarind purée

6–8 boneless, skinless duck breasts
1 red onion, sliced
125 ml (4 fl oz/½ cup) white vinegar
500 ml (17 fl oz/2 cups) coconut milk
2 tablespoons coriander (cilantro) leaves

serves 6

method To make the curry paste, place all the ingredients in a food processor and process to a thick paste. Put aside.

Trim any excess fat from the duck breasts, then place, skin side down, in a large saucepan and cook over medium heat for 10 minutes, or until the skin is brown and any remaining fat has melted. Turn the fillets over and cook for 5 minutes, or until tender. Remove and drain on paper towels.

Reserve 1 tablespoon duck fat, discarding the remaining fat. Add the onion and cook for 5 minutes, then add the curry paste and stir over low heat for 10 minutes, or until fragrant.

Return the duck to the pan and stir to coat with the paste. Stir in the vinegar, coconut milk, 1 teaspoon salt and 125 ml (4 fl oz/½ cup) water. Simmer, covered, for 45 minutes, or until the duck breasts are tender. Stir in the coriander just prior to serving. Serve with steamed rice and naan bread.

100 EASY RECIPES ONE-POTS

tomato chicken casserole

1.5 kg (3 lb 5 oz) chicken pieces
40 g (1½ oz) butter
1 tablespoon oil
1 large onion, chopped
2 garlic cloves, chopped
1 small green capsicum (pepper), chopped
150 g (5½ oz) mushrooms, thickly sliced
1 tablespoon plain (all-purpose) flour
250 ml (9 fl oz/1 cup) white wine
1 tablespoon white wine vinegar
4 tomatoes, peeled, seeded and chopped
2 tablespoons tomato paste (concentrated purée)
90 g (3 oz/½ cup) small black olives
2 large handfuls flat-leaf (Italian) parsley, chopped

serves 4

method Preheat the oven to 180°C (350°F/Gas 4). Remove the excess fat from the chicken pieces and pat dry with paper towels. Heat 2 teaspoons of the butter and 2 teaspoons of the oil in a large flameproof casserole dish. Cook half the chicken over high heat until browned all over, then set aside. Heat another 2 teaspoons of the butter and the remaining oil, and cook the remaining chicken. Set aside.

Heat the remaining butter in the casserole dish and cook the onion and garlic for 2–3 minutes over medium–high heat. Add the capsicum and mushroom, and cook, stirring, for 3 minutes. Stir in the flour and cook for 1 minute. Add the wine, vinegar, tomato and tomato paste, and cook, stirring, for 2 minutes, or until slightly thickened.

Return the chicken to the casserole dish and make sure it is covered by the tomato and onion mixture. Place in the oven and cook, covered, for 1 hour, or until the chicken is tender. Stir in the olives and parsley. Season with salt and freshly cracked black pepper, and serve with pasta.

green chicken curry

500 ml (17 fl oz/2 cups) coconut cream (do not shake the tin—see Note)
90 g (3 oz/⅓ cup) Thai green curry paste
2 tablespoons grated palm sugar (jaggery) or soft brown sugar
2 tablespoons fish sauce
4 makrut (kaffir lime) leaves, finely shredded
1 kg (2 lb 4 oz) boneless, skinless chicken thigh or breasts, cut into thick strips
200 g (7 oz) bamboo shoots, trimmed and cut into thick strips
100 g (3½ oz) snake (yard-long) beans, trimmed and cut into 5 cm (2 inch) lengths
1 handful basil leaves

serves 4–6

method Place 125 ml (4 fl oz/½ cup) of the thick coconut cream from the top of the tin in a wok, and bring to the boil. Add the curry paste, then reduce the heat and simmer for 15 minutes, or until fragrant and the oil starts to separate from the cream. Add the palm sugar, fish sauce and makrut leaves to the pan.

Stir in the remaining coconut cream and the chicken, bamboo shoots and beans, and simmer for 15 minutes, or until the chicken is tender. Stir in the basil and serve with rice.

note *Do not shake the tin of coconut cream because good-quality coconut cream has a layer of very thick cream at the top that has separated from the rest of the cream. This has a higher fat content, which causes it to split or separate more readily than the rest of the coconut cream.*

chicken, artichoke and broad bean stew

155 g (5½ oz/1 cup) frozen broad (fava) beans
8 chicken thighs (skin removed, optional)
60 g (2 oz/½ cup) seasoned plain
(all-purpose) flour
2 tablespoons oil
1 large red onion, cut into small wedges
125 ml (4 fl oz/½ cup) dry white wine
310 ml (11 fl oz/1¼ cups) chicken stock
2 teaspoons finely chopped fresh rosemary
335 g (12 oz) marinated artichokes, well
drained and quartered
800 g (1 lb 12 oz) potatoes, cut into large
cubes
60 g (2 oz) butter

serves 4

method Remove the skins from the broad beans. Coat the chicken in the flour, shaking off the excess. Heat the oil in a saucepan or flameproof casserole dish, then brown the chicken in two batches on all sides over medium heat. Remove and drain on paper towels.

Add the onion to the pan and cook for 3–4 minutes, or until soft but not brown. Increase the heat to high, pour in the wine and boil for 2 minutes, or until reduced to a syrup. Stir in 250 ml (9 fl oz/1 cup) of the stock and bring just to the boil, then return the chicken to the pan with the rosemary. Reduce the heat to low and simmer, covered, for 45 minutes.

Add the artichokes to the pan, increase the heat to high and return to the boil. Reduce to a simmer and cook, uncovered, for 10–15 minutes. Add the beans and cook for a further 5 minutes.

Meanwhile, cook the potato in a saucepan of boiling water for 15–20 minutes, or until tender. Drain, then return to the pan. Add the butter and the remaining stock, and mash with a potato masher. Serve on the side of the stew.

beef and veal

vietnamese beef noodle soup

400 g (14 oz) rump steak, trimmed
1 litre (35 fl oz/4 cups) beef stock
½ onion
1 star anise
1 cinnamon stick
1 tablespoon fish sauce
pinch ground white pepper
200 g (7 oz) fresh thin round rice noodles
2 spring onions (scallions), thinly sliced
30 mint leaves
90 g (3 oz/1 cup) bean sprouts, trimmed
1 small white onion, thinly sliced
1 small red chilli, thinly sliced

serves 4

method Wrap the meat in plastic wrap and freeze for 30–40 minutes, or until partially frozen. Thinly slice the meat across the grain.

Place the stock in a large heavy-based saucepan with the onion half, star anise, cinnamon stick, fish sauce, white pepper and 500 ml (17 fl oz/2 cups) water, and bring to the boil over high heat. Reduce the heat to low– medium and simmer, covered, for 20 minutes. Discard the onion, star anise and cinnamon stick.

Meanwhile, cover the noodles with boiling water and gently separate. Drain and refresh with cold water. Divide the noodles and spring onion among the serving bowls. Top with equal amounts of beef, mint leaves, bean sprouts, onion slices and chilli. Ladle the simmering broth into the bowls, and serve.

note *It is important that the broth is kept hot as the heat will cook the slices of beef.*

100 EASY RECIPES ONE-POTS

hot beef borscht

500 g (1 lb 2 oz) stewing beef, cut into cubes
500 g (1 lb 2 oz) beetroot (beets)
1 onion, finely chopped
1 carrot, cut into short strips
1 parsnip, cut into short strips
75 g (2½ oz/1 cup) finely shredded cabbage
sour cream, to serve
snipped chives, to serve

serves 4–6

method Put the beef and 1 litre (35 fl oz/4 cups) water in a large heavy-based saucepan, and bring slowly to the boil. Reduce the heat, cover and simmer for 1 hour. Skim the surface of the stock to remove the fat as required.

Cut the stems from the beetroot, wash well and place in a large, heavy-based saucepan with 1 litre (35 fl oz/4 cups) water. Bring to the boil, then reduce the heat and simmer for 40 minutes, or until the beetroot is tender. Drain, reserving 250 ml (9 fl oz /1 cup) of the liquid. Allow to cool, then peel and grate the beetroot.

Remove the meat from the stock and cool. Skim any remaining fat from the surface of the stock. Return the meat to the stock and add the onion, carrot, parsnip, beetroot and reserved beetroot liquid. Bring to the boil, reduce the heat, cover and simmer for 45 minutes.

Stir in the cabbage and simmer for a further 15 minutes. Season to taste. Serve with the sour cream and chives.

beef and peppercorn stew

1 kg (2 lb 4 oz) chuck steak, cut into 3 cm
   (1¼ inch) cubes
2 teaspoons cracked black peppercorns
40 g (1½ oz) butter
2 tablespoons oil
1 large onion, thinly sliced
2 garlic cloves, sliced
1½ tablespoons plain (all-purpose) flour
2 tablespoons brandy
750 ml (26 fl oz/3 cups) beef stock
1 tablespoon worcestershire sauce
2 teaspoons dijon mustard
500 g (1 lb 2 oz) baby new potatoes
60 ml (2 fl oz/¼ cup) cream
2 tablespoons chopped parsley

serves 4

method Toss the steak in the peppercorns. Heat half the butter and half the oil in a large heavy-based saucepan. Brown half the steak over high heat, then remove and set aside. Heat the remaining butter and oil, and brown the remaining steak. Remove from the pan and set aside.

Add the onion and garlic to the pan and cook, stirring, until the onion is golden. Add the flour and stir until browned. Remove from the heat.

Combine the brandy, beef stock, worcestershire sauce and mustard, and gradually stir into the onion mixture. Return to the heat, add the steak and any juices, then simmer, covered, for 1¼ hours.

Add the potatoes and simmer, uncovered, for a further 30 minutes, or until the meat and potatoes are tender. Stir in the cream and parsley, and season to taste with salt and freshly ground black pepper. This is delicious served with a green salad.

100 EASY RECIPES ONE-POTS

chilli con carne

185 g (6½ oz) dried black-eyed peas
1½ tablespoons oil
900 g (2 lb) trimmed chuck steak, cut into chunks
3 onions, thinly sliced
2 garlic cloves, chopped
2 teaspoons ground cumin
1 tablespoon paprika
½ teaspoon allspice powder
1–2 teaspoons chilli powder
650 g (1 lb 7 oz) tomatoes, peeled, seeded and finely chopped
1 tablespoon soft brown sugar
1 tablespoon red wine vinegar

serves 6

method Put the peas in a bowl, cover with plenty of water and leave to soak overnight. Drain well.

Heat 1 tablespoon of the oil in a large heavy-based saucepan and cook the meat in two batches over medium–high heat for 2 minutes, or until well browned. Remove from the pan.

Pour the rest of the oil into the saucepan and add the onion. Cook over medium heat for 5 minutes, or until translucent. Add the garlic and spices and cook, stirring, for 1 minute, or until aromatic. Add 500 ml (17 fl oz/2 cups) water and stir in.

Return the meat to the pan with the peas and tomato. Bring to the boil, then reduce the heat to low and simmer, partially covered, for 2 hours, or until the meat is tender and the chilli con carne is thick and dryish, stirring occasionally. Towards the end of the cooking time the mixture may start to catch, so add a little water if necessary. Stir through the sugar and vinegar, and season with salt to taste. This is delicious served with flour tortillas and grated cheddar cheese.

beef and lentil curry

3–4 small dried red chillies
60 ml (2 fl oz/¼ cup) oil
2 red onions, cut into thin wedges
4 garlic cloves, finely chopped
1 tablespoon grated fresh ginger
1 tablespoon garam masala
3 cardamom pods, lightly crushed
1 cinnamon stick
2 teaspoons ground turmeric
750 g (1 lb 10 oz) chuck steak, cut into cubes
400 g (14 oz) tin chopped tomatoes
95 g (3 oz/½ cup) brown or green lentils
125 g (4½ oz/½ cup) red lentils
200 g (7 oz) pumpkin (winter squash), diced
150 g (5½ oz) eggplant (aubergine), diced
125 g (4½ oz) baby English spinach
1 tablespoon tamarind purée
2 tablespoons grated palm sugar (jaggery)
  or soft brown sugar

serves 6

method Soak the chillies in boiling water for 10 minutes, then drain and finely chop.

Heat the oil in a large saucepan. Add the onion and cook, stirring, over medium heat for 5 minutes, or until soft. Add the garlic and ginger, and cook for a further 2 minutes.

Add the chilli, garam masala, cardamom pods, cinnamon, turmeric and ½ teaspoon black pepper. Cook, stirring, for 2 minutes, or until fragrant. Add beef and stir constantly for 3–4 minutes, or until meat is coated in spices.

Add the tomato, lentils, 1 teaspoon salt and 750 ml (26 fl oz/3 cups) water. Simmer, covered, for 1 hour until tender. Stir often to prevent burning. Add extra water, if needed.

Add the pumpkin and eggplant to pan, and cook, covered, for 20 minutes, or until tender. Stir in the spinach, tamarind and palm sugar, and cook for a further 10 minutes.

paprika veal with caraway noodles

60 ml (2 fl oz/¼ cup) oil
1 kg (2 lb 4 oz) veal shoulder, diced
1 large onion, thinly sliced
3 garlic cloves, finely chopped
60 g (2 oz/¼ cup) Hungarian paprika
½ teaspoon caraway seeds
2 x 400 g (14 oz) tins chopped tomatoes,
one drained
350 g (12 oz) fresh fettuccine
40 g (1½ oz) butter, softened

serves 4

method Heat half the oil in a large saucepan over medium–high heat, then brown the veal in batches for 3 minutes per batch. Remove the veal from the pan and set aside with any pan juices.

Add the remaining oil to the pan and sauté the onion and garlic over medium heat for 5 minutes, or until softened. Add the paprika and ¼ teaspoon of the caraway seeds, and stir for 30 seconds.

Add all the chopped tomatoes and their liquid plus 125 ml (4 fl oz/½ cup) water. Return the veal to the pan with any juices, increase the heat to high and bring to the boil. Reduce the heat to low, then cover and simmer for 1¼ hours, or until the meat is tender and the sauce has reduced and thickened.

About 15 minutes before the veal is ready, cook the pasta in a large saucepan of rapidly boiling salted water according to the packet instructions until al dente. Drain, then return to the pan. Stir in the butter and the remaining caraway seeds. Serve immediately with the paprika veal.

beef rendang

2 onions, roughly chopped
2 garlic cloves, crushed
400 ml (14 fl oz) tin coconut milk
2 teaspoons ground coriander seeds
½ teaspoon ground fennel seeds
2 teaspoons ground cumin seeds
¼ teaspoon ground cloves
1.5 kg (3 lb 5 oz) chuck steak, cut into 3 cm
    (1¼ inch) cubes
4–6 small fresh red chillies, chopped
1 tablespoon lemon juice
1 lemongrass stem (white part only), bruised,
    cut lengthways
2 teaspoons grated palm sugar (jaggery) or
    soft brown sugar
coriander (cilantro) sprigs, to garnish

serves 6

method Place the coconut milk in a large saucepan and bring to the boil, then reduce the heat to medium and cook, stirring occasionally, for 15 minutes, or until the milk has reduced by half and the oil has separated. Do not allow the milk to brown.

Add the coriander seeds, fennel, cumin and cloves to the pan, and stir for 1 minute. Add the meat and cook for 2 minutes, or until it changes colour. Add the onion mixture, chilli, lemon juice, lemongrass and palm sugar. Cook, covered, over medium heat for 2 hours, or until the liquid has reduced and the mixture has thickened. Stir frequently to prevent it sticking to the bottom of the pan.

Uncover and continue cooking until the oil from the coconut milk begins to emerge again, letting the curry develop. Be careful that it does not burn. The curry is cooked when it is brown and dry. Serve with rice and coriander sprigs.

steak and kidney stew

1 kg (2 lb 4 oz) chuck steak, trimmed
8 lamb kidneys
60 ml (2 fl oz/¼ cup) oil
1 bacon slice, rind removed, cut into long,
thin strips
40 g (1½ oz) butter
1 large onion, chopped
300 g (10½ oz) button mushrooms, halved
250 ml (9 fl oz/1 cup) Muscat
2–3 garlic cloves, crushed
¼ teaspoon ground allspice
½ teaspoon paprika
2 teaspoons coriander seeds, lightly crushed
1 tablespoon wholegrain mustard
250 ml (9 fl oz/1 cup) beef stock
2–3 tablespoons soft brown sugar
1–2 teaspoons thyme leaves
1–2 teaspoons rosemary chopped

serves 4–6

method Cut the steak into 2–3 cm (1 inch) cubes. Cut the kidneys in half, remove the core and any fat, then slice them in half again.

Heat 1 teaspoon of the oil in a large heavy-based saucepan. Add the bacon and cook over medium heat until just crisp. Remove and then set aside.

Heat 2 tablespoons of the oil and 30 g (1 oz) of the butter in the pan. Brown the steak cubes in batches, then set aside.

Add the onion to the pan and cook for 3 minutes, or until soft and golden. Add the mushrooms and cook, stirring, for 3 minutes, until starting to brown. Stir in half the Muscat and simmer for 3–4 minutes. Remove and set to the side.

Add the remaining oil and butter to the pan. Stir in the garlic, allspice, paprika and coriander seeds, and cook for 1 minute. Add the kidney and cook until just starting to brown. Stir in the mustard and remaining Muscat, and simmer for 2 minutes.

Stir in the bacon, steak, and onion and mushroom mixture. Stir in the stock, bring to the boil, then reduce the heat, cover and simmer for 1 hour. Add the sugar. Simmer, covered, for 40 minutes, then uncovered for 20 minutes, stirring in the herbs during the last 10 minutes.

red beef and eggplant curry

250 ml (9 fl oz) tin coconut cream (do not
   shake the tin)
2 tablespoons Thai red curry paste
500 g (1 lb 2 oz) round or topside steak, cut
   into strips (see Note)
2 tablespoons fish sauce
1 tablespoon grated palm sugar (jaggery) or
   soft brown sugar
5 makrut (kaffir lime) leaves, halved
500 ml (17 fl oz/2 cups) coconut milk
8 Thai eggplants (aubergines), halved
2 tablespoons finely shredded Thai basil leaves

serves 4

method Place the thick coconut cream from the top of the tin in a wok and bring to the boil. Boil for 10 minutes, or until the oil starts to separate. Add the curry paste and simmer, stirring to prevent it sticking to the bottom, for 5 minutes, or until fragrant.

Add the meat and cook, stirring, for 3–5 minutes, or until it changes colour. Add the fish sauce, palm sugar, makrut leaves, coconut milk and remaining coconut cream, and simmer for 1 hour, or until the meat is tender and the sauce has slightly thickened.

Add the eggplant and cook for 10 minutes, or until tender. If the sauce is too thick, add a little water. Stir in half the shredded basil. Garnish with the remaining basil leaves and serve with steamed rice.

note *Cut the meat into 5 x 5 x 2 cm (2 x 2 x ¾ inch) pieces, then cut across the grain at a 45° angle into 5 mm (¼ inch) thick slices.*

japanese-style sukiyaki

sauce

½–1 teaspoon dashi granules
80 ml (2½ fl oz/⅓ cup) soy sauce
2 tablespoons sake (dry rice wine)
2 tablespoons mirin (sweet rice wine)
1 tablespoon caster (superfine) sugar

300 g (10½ oz) shirataki noodles
50 g (2 oz) lard
5 large spring onions (scallions), cut into 1 cm
(½ inch) slices on the diagonal
16 fresh shiitake mushrooms, cut into smaller
pieces if large
800 g (1 lb 12 oz) rump steak, thinly sliced
across the grain
100 g (3½ oz) watercress, trimmed
4 eggs (optional)

serves 4

method To make the sauce, dissolve the dashi granules in 125 ml (4 fl oz/¹/₂ cup) water. Add the soy sauce, sake, mirin and sugar, and stir until combined.

Drain the noodles, then soak them in boiling water for 2 minutes. Rinse in cold water and drain well.

Melt the lard in a large frying pan over medium heat. Cook the spring onion, mushrooms and beef in batches, stirring, for 1–2 minutes each batch, or until just brown. Return the meat, spring onion and mushrooms to the pan, then add the sauce and watercress. Cook for 1 minute, or until heated through and the watercress has wilted—the sauce needs to just cover the ingredients but not drown them.

To serve, divide the noodles among four serving bowls and spoon the sauce evenly over the top. If desired, crack an egg into each bowl and break up through the sauce using chopsticks until it partially cooks.

chinese beef in soy

700 g (1 lb 9 oz) chuck steak, trimmed and cut
   into 2 cm (¾ inch) cubes
80 ml (2½ fl oz/⅓ cup) dark soy sauce
2 tablespoons honey
1 tablespoon wine vinegar
60 ml (2 fl oz/¼ cup) soya bean oil, or
   cooking oil
4 garlic cloves, chopped
8 spring onions (scallions), thinly sliced
1 tablespoon finely grated fresh ginger
2 star anise
½ teaspoon ground cloves
375 ml (13 fl oz/1½ cups) beef stock
125 ml (4 fl oz/½ cup) red wine
sliced spring onions (scallions), extra, to garnish

serves 4

method Place the meat in a non-metallic dish. Combine the soy sauce, honey and vinegar in a small bowl, then pour over the meat. Cover with plastic wrap and marinate for at least 2 hours, or preferably overnight. Drain, reserving the marinade, and pat the cubes dry.

Place 1 tablespoon of the oil in a saucepan and brown the meat in 3 batches, for 3–4 minutes per batch—add another tablespoon of oil, if necessary. Remove the meat. Add the remaining oil and fry the garlic, spring onion, ginger, star anise and cloves for 1–2 minutes, or until fragrant.

Return all the meat to the pan, and add the reserved marinade, stock and wine. Bring to the boil, then reduce the heat and simmer, covered, for 1¼ hours. Cook, uncovered, for a further 15 minutes, or until the sauce is syrupy and the meat is tender.

Garnish with the extra sliced spring onion and serve immediately with steamed rice.

corned beef

1 tablespoon oil
1.5 kg (3 lb 5 oz) piece corned silverside, trimmed
1 tablespoon white vinegar
1 tablespoon soft brown sugar
4 cloves
4 black peppercorns
2 bay leaves
1 garlic clove, crushed
1 large parsley sprig
4 carrots
4 potatoes
6 small onions

onion sauce

30 g (1 oz) butter
2 white onions, chopped
2 tablespoons plain (all-purpose) flour
330ml (11 fl oz/1⅓ cups) full-cream (whole) milk

horseradish cream

60 ml (2 fl oz/¼ cup) horseradish relish
1 tablespoon white vinegar
125 ml (4 fl oz/½ cup) cream

serves 6–8

method Heat the oil in a deep, heavy-based saucepan. Cook the meat over medium–high heat, turning until well browned all over. Remove the pan from the heat and add the vinegar, sugar, cloves, peppercorns, bay leaves, garlic and parsley sprig.

Pour over enough water to cover. Cover and return to the heat, reduce the heat and bring slowly to a simmering point. Then simmer for a further 30 minutes.

Cut the carrots and potatoes into large pieces and add to the pan with the onions. Simmer, covered, for 1 hour, or until tender. Remove the vegetables and keep warm. Reserve 125 ml (4 fl oz/½ cup) of the cooking liquid.

Meanwhile to make the onion sauce, heat the butter in a small saucepan. Cook the onion gently for 10 minutes, or until soft but not browned. Transfer the onion to a bowl. Add the flour to the pan and stir over low heat for 2 minutes, or until the flour is lightly golden. Gradually add the milk and the reserved cooking liquid, and stir until the sauce boils and thickens. Boil for 1 minute, then remove from the heat and stir in the onion. Season to taste.

To make the horseradish cream, combine all of the ingredients in a bowl until smooth.

Drain the meat from the pan, discarding the remaining liquid and spices. Slice the meat, and serve it with the vegetables, onion sauce and horseradish cream. Garnish with bay leaves if desired.

japanese beef hotpot

300 g (10½ oz) beef fillet, trimmed
1.5 litres (52 fl oz/6 cups) chicken stock
2 cm x 6 cm (¾ inch x 2½ inch) piece fresh
　ginger, thinly sliced
80 ml (2½ fl oz/⅓ cup) light soy sauce
2 tablespoons mirin
1 teaspoon sesame oil
200 g (7 oz) fresh udon noodles
150 g (5½ oz) English spinach, stems removed,
　thinly sliced
400 g (14 oz) cabbage, finely shredded
100 g (3½ oz) fresh shiitake mushrooms, stems
　removed and caps thinly sliced
200 g (7 oz) firm tofu, cut into 2 cm (¾ inch)
　cubes
80 ml (2½ fl oz/⅓ cup) ponzu sauce, or 60 ml
　(2 fl oz/¼ cup) soy sauce combined with
　1 tablespoon lemon juice

serves 4

method Wrap the beef fillet in plastic wrap and freeze for 40 minutes, or until it begins to harden. Remove and slice as thinly as possible across the grain.

Place the stock, ginger, soy sauce, mirin and sesame oil in a 2.5 litre (87 fl oz/10 cup) flameproof casserole dish or hotpot over medium heat, and simmer for 3 minutes. Separate the noodles gently with chopsticks, add to the stock and cook for 1–2 minutes. Add the spinach, cabbage, mushrooms and tofu, and simmer for 1 minute, or until the leaves have wilted.

Divide the noodles among four serving bowls using tongs, and top with the beef slices, vegetables and tofu. Ladle the hot stock on top and serve the ponzu sauce on the side.

note *Traditionally, raw beef slices are arranged on a plate with the tofu, mushrooms, vegetables and noodles. The stock and seasoning are heated on a portable gas flame at the table. Guests dip the meat and vegetables in the hot stock and eat as they go, dipping into the sauce. The noodles are added at the end and served with the broth.*

osso bucco

12 meaty pieces veal shank, osso bucco style
40 g (1½ oz/⅓ cup) seasoned plain
(all-purpose) flour
20 g (¾ oz) butter
80 ml (2½ fl oz/⅓ cup) olive oil
1 onion, diced
1 carrot, diced
1 celery stalk, diced
1 bay leaf
1 garlic clove, crushed
500 ml (17 fl oz/2 cups) veal or chicken stock
250ml (9 fl oz/1 cup) white wine
80 ml (2½ fl oz/⅓ cup) lemon juice

gremolata

4 tablespoons flat-leaf (Italian) parsley
2 garlic cloves, finely chopped
1 tablespoon grated lemon zest

serves 4–6

method Lightly dust the veal shanks in the seasoned flour. Put the butter and 60 ml (2 fl oz/¼ cup) of the oil in a large deep-sided frying pan over high heat and heat until sizzling. Add the veal and cook in batches for 5 minutes, or until brown all over. Remove from the pan.

Heat the remaining oil in the pan, add the onion, carrot, celery and bay leaf, and cook for 10 minutes, or until softened and starting to brown. Add the garlic, stock, wine and lemon juice, and stir to combine, scraping the bottom of the pan to remove any sediment. Return the veal to the pan, bring to the boil, then reduce the heat to low, cover and simmer for 1½–2 hours, or until the veal is very tender and falling off the bone and the sauce has reduced. Season to taste.

To make the gremolata, finely chop the parsley and mix together with the garlic and lemon zest. Sprinkle over just before serving. Serve with soft polenta.

madras beef curry

1 tablespoon oil or ghee
1 onion, chopped
55–90 g (2–3 oz/¼– ⅓ cup) Madras curry paste
1 kg (2 lb 4 oz) skirt or chuck steak, trimmed of
    fat and cut into 2.5 cm (1 inch) cubes
60 g (2 oz/¼ cup) tomato paste
    (concentrated purée)
250 ml (9 fl oz/1 cup) beef stock
coriander (cilantro) sprigs, to garnish

serves 4

method Heat the oil in a large frying pan, add the onion and cook over medium heat for about 10 minutes, or until browned. Add the curry paste and stir for 1 minute, or until fragrant. Then add the meat and cook, stirring, until coated with the curry paste.

Stir in the tomato paste and stock. Reduce the heat and simmer, covered, for 1¼ hours, Add more stock or water if necessary. Simmer uncovered for 15 minutes, or until the meat is tender. Garnish with coriander and serve with steamed rice.

spiced beef and potatoes

2 onions, chopped
2 garlic cloves, chopped
2 teaspoons grated lemon zest
2 small red chillies, chopped
2 teaspoons ground coriander
2 teaspoons ground cumin
1 teaspoon ground turmeric
½ teaspoon ground cardamom
1 teaspoon garam masala

2 tablespoons oil
1 kg (2 lb 4 oz) lean chuck steak, cut into
3 cm (1¼ inch) cubes
185 ml (6 fl oz/¾ cup) coconut cream
1 tablespoon tamarind sauce
500 g (1 lb 2 oz) baby potatoes, halved

serves 4

method To make the spice paste, combine all the ingredients in a food processor, and process for 1 minute, or until very finely chopped.

Heat the oil in a heavy-based saucepan. Cook the meat quickly in small batches over medium–high heat until well browned. Drain meat on paper towels.

Add the spice paste to the pan and stir over medium heat for 2 minutes. Return the meat to the pan with the coconut cream, tamarind sauce and 125 ml (4 fl oz/½ cup) water, and bring to the boil. Reduce the heat to a simmer and cook, covered, for 30 minutes, stirring occasionally.

Add the potato and cook, covered, for 30 minutes. Remove the lid and cook for another 30 minutes, or until the meat is tender and almost all of the liquid has evaporated.

beef pot roast

300 g (10½ oz) baby brown onions
2 carrots
3 parsnips, peeled
40 g (1½ oz) butter
1–1.5 kg (2 lb 4 oz–3 lb 5 oz) eye of silverside,
    trimmed of fat (see Note)
60 ml (2 fl oz/¼ cup) dry red wine
1 large tomato, finely chopped
250 ml (9 fl oz/1 cup) beef stock
mild or hot English mustard, to serve

serves 6

method Put the onions in a heatproof bowl and cover with boiling water. Leave for 1 minute, then drain well. Allow them to cool, then peel off the skins.

Cut the carrots and parsnips in half lengthways, then into even-sized pieces. Heat half the butter in a large heavy-based saucepan that will tightly fit the meat (it will shrink during cooking), add the onions, carrot and parsnip, and cook, stirring, over medium–high heat until browned. Remove from the pan. Add the remaining butter to the pan and add the meat, browning well all over. Increase the heat to high and pour in the wine. Bring to the boil, then add the tomato and stock. Return to the boil, then reduce the heat to low, cover and simmer for 2 hours, turning once. Add the vegetables and simmer, covered, for 1 hour.

Remove the meat from the pan and put it on a board ready for carving. Cover with foil and leave it to stand while finishing the sauce.

Increase the heat to high and boil the pan juices with the vegetables for 10 minutes to reduce and thicken slightly. Skim off any excess fat, and taste before seasoning. Slice the meat and arrange on a serving platter or individual serving plates with the vegetables. Drizzle generously with the pan juices. Serve with mustard and pepper.

note *Eye of silverside is a tender, long-shaped cut of silverside that carves easily into serving-sized pieces. A regular piece of silverside or topside may be substituted.*

100 EASY RECIPES ONE-POTS

beef stroganoff

1 kg (2 lb 4 oz) piece rump steak, trimmed
40 g (1½ oz/⅓ cup) plain (all-purpose) flour
¼ teaspoon ground black pepper
60 ml (2 fl oz/¼ cup) olive oil
1 large onion, chopped
500 g (1 lb 2 oz) baby mushrooms
1 tablespoon sweet paprika
1 tablespoon tomato paste
2 teaspoons French mustard
125 ml (4 fl oz/½ cup) dry white wine
60 ml (2 fl oz/¼ cup) chicken stock
185 g (6½ oz/¾ cup) sour cream
1 tablespoon finely chopped flat-leaf (Italian)
parsley

serves 6

method Slice the meat across the grain into short, thin pieces. Combine the flour and pepper. Toss the meat in the seasoned flour, shaking off the excess.

Heat 2 tablespoons of the oil in a heavy-based saucepan. Cook the meat quickly in small batches over medium–high heat until well browned. Drain on paper towels.

Heat the remaining oil in the pan. Cook the onion over medium heat for 3 minutes, or until softened. Add the mushrooms and stir for 5 minutes.

Add the paprika, tomato paste, mustard, wine and stock to the pan, and bring to the boil. Reduce the heat and simmer for 5 minutes, uncovered, stirring occasionally. Return the meat to the pan along with the sour cream, and stir until combined and just heated through. Sprinkle with the chopped parsley just before serving.

thai beef and pumpkin curry

2 tablespoons oil
750 g (1 lb 10 oz) blade steak, thinly sliced
90 g (3 oz/⅓ cup) Massaman curry paste
2 garlic cloves, finely chopped
1 onion, sliced lengthways
6 curry leaves, torn
750 ml (26 fl oz/3 cups) coconut milk
450 g (1 lb) butternut pumpkin (squash),
    roughly diced
2 tablespoons chopped unsalted peanuts
1 tablespoon grated palm sugar (jaggery) or
    soft brown sugar
2 tablespoons tamarind purée
2 tablespoons fish sauce
curry leaves, extra, to garnish

serves 6

method Heat a wok or frying pan over high heat. Add the oil and swirl to coat the side. Add the meat in batches and cook for 5 minutes, or until browned. Remove the meat from the wok.

Add the curry paste, garlic, onion and curry leaves to the wok, and stir to coat. Return the meat to the wok and cook, stirring, over medium heat for 2 minutes.

Add the coconut milk to the wok, then reduce the heat to low and gently simmer for 45 minutes. Add the pumpkin and simmer for 25–30 minutes, or until the meat and the pumpkin are tender and the sauce has thickened.

Stir in the peanuts, palm sugar, tamarind purée and fish sauce, and simmer for 1 minute. Garnish with curry leaves and season with cracked black pepper. Serve with steamed rice.

100 EASY RECIPES ONE-POTS

creamy veal with mushrooms

750 g (1 lb 10 oz) veal steaks, cut into 1 cm
(½ inch) strips
30 g (1 oz/¼ cup) plain (all-purpose) flour
30 g (1 oz) butter
1 garlic clove, crushed
1 tablespoon dijon mustard
250 ml (9 fl oz/1 cup) cream
125 ml (4 fl oz/½ cup) white wine
1 tablespoon chopped fresh thyme
250 ml (9 fl oz/1 cup) chicken stock
375 g (13 oz) button mushrooms, halved

serves 4

method Toss the meat in the flour (inside a plastic bag prevents mess), shaking off the excess. Heat the butter and garlic in a large frying pan. Add the meat and cook quickly in small batches over medium heat until well browned. Drain thoroughly on paper towels.

Brown the mushrooms in the pan, then add the mustard, cream, wine, thyme and chicken stock. Bring to the boil, then reduce the heat and simmer, covered, for 10–15 minutes, stirring occasionally, until the sauce thickens.

Add the veal and cook for a further 3–5 minutes, or until the meat is tender and warmed through. Delicious served with pasta and steamed vegetables.

beef bourguignon

1 kg (2 lb 4 oz) stewing beef, cubed
30 g (1 oz/¼ cup) seasoned plain (all-purpose) flour
1 tablespoon oil
150 g (5½ oz) bacon slices, diced
8 bulb spring onions (scallions), greens trimmed to 2 cm (¾ inch)
200 g (7 oz) button mushrooms
500 ml (17 fl oz/2 cups) red wine
2 tablespoons tomato paste (concentrated purée)
500 ml (17 fl oz/2 cups) beef stock
1 bouquet garni (see Note)

serves 4

method Toss the beef in the seasoned flour until evenly coated, shaking off any excess. Heat the oil in a large saucepan over high heat. Cook the beef in three batches for about 3 minutes, or until well browned all over, adding a little extra oil as needed. Remove from the pan.

Add the bacon to the pan and cook for 2 minutes, or until browned. Remove with a slotted spoon and add to the beef. Add the spring onions and mushrooms, and cook for 5 minutes, or until the onions are browned. Remove.

Slowly pour the red wine into the pan, scraping up any sediment from the bottom with a wooden spoon. Stir in the tomato paste and stock. Add the bouquet garni and return the beef, bacon and any juices. Bring to the boil, then reduce the heat and simmer for 45 minutes. Return the spring onions and mushrooms to the pan. Cook for 1 hour, or until the meat is very tender and the sauce is glossy. Serve with steamed new potatoes or mash.

note *To make a bouquet garni, wrap the green part of a leek around a bay leaf, a sprig of thyme, a sprig of parsley and celery leaves, and tie with string. The combination of herbs can be varied according to taste.*

french-style beef pot roast

2 tablespoons oil
2 kg (4 lb 8 oz) rolled beef brisket, trimmed
750 ml (26 fl oz/3 cups) beef stock
250 ml (9 fl oz/1 cup) red wine
60 ml (2 fl oz/¼ cup) brandy
2 onions, quartered
3 garlic cloves, crushed
3 tomatoes, peeled, seeded and chopped
2 bay leaves
1 large handful chopped parsley
2 tablespoons thyme leaves
12 pitted black olives
6 small carrots, thickly sliced
2 tablespoons plain (all-purpose) flour

serves 6

method Heat the oil in a deep heavy-based saucepan. Cook the meat over medium–high heat until browned all over, then remove from the heat.

Add the stock to the pan with the wine, brandy, onion, garlic, tomato, bay leaves, parsley and thyme. Cover and bring to simmering point over low heat. Simmer for 1½ hours.

Add the olives and carrot, and cook for 30 minutes. Remove the meat and leave it in a warm place, and covered with foil, for 10 minutes before slicing.

Combine the flour and 60 ml (2 fl oz/¼ cup) water to make a smooth paste. Add to the sauce, stir over medium heat until the sauce thickens, and cook for 3 minutes. Pour over the sliced meat to serve.

beef in beer with capers

1 kg (2 lb 4 oz) gravy beef
seasoned plain (all-purpose) flour
olive oil, for cooking
4 garlic cloves, finely chopped
500 ml (17 fl oz/2 cups) beef stock
375 ml (13 fl oz/1½ cups) beer
2 onions, chopped
3 bay leaves
55 g (2 oz/⅓ cup) stuffed or pitted green
   olives, sliced
6 anchovies
2 tablespoons capers, drained

serves 4–6

method Cut the beef into 4 cm (1½ inch) chunks. Lightly coat in the flour. Heat 60 ml (2 fl oz/ ¼ cup) of oil in a deep heavy-based saucepan, add the garlic, then brown the beef over a high heat.

Add the stock, beer, onion and bay leaves, season well and bring to the boil. Reduce the heat and gently simmer, covered, for 2½ hours, stirring about three times during cooking. Remove the lid and simmer for 30 minutes more. Stir, then mix in the olives.

Heat 2 teaspoons of oil in a small saucepan. Add the anchovies and capers, gently breaking up the anchovies. Cook over medium heat for 4 minutes, or until brown and crisp. To serve, place the meat on serving plates, drizzle with the sauce, sprinkle with anchovies and capers, and season with salt and freshly cracked black pepper.

note *The capers should be squeezed very dry before being added to the pan, or they will spit in the hot oil.*

massaman beef curry

1 tablespoon tamarind pulp
2 tablespoons oil
750 g (1 lb 10 oz) lean stewing beef, cubed
500 ml (17 fl oz/2 cups) coconut milk
4 cardamom pods, bruised
500 ml (17 fl oz/2 cups) coconut cream
2–3 tablespoons Massaman curry paste
8 baby onions, peeled (see Note)
8 baby potatoes, peeled and quartered
(see Note)
2 tablespoons fish sauce
2 tablespoons grated palm sugar (jaggery) or
soft brown sugar
80 g (3 oz/½ cup) unsalted peanuts, roasted
and ground
coriander (cilantro) leaves, to garnish

serves 4

method Place the tamarind pulp and ½ cup (125 ml/4 fl oz) boiling water in a bowl and set aside to cool. When cool, mash the pulp to dissolve in the water, then strain and reserve the liquid. Discard the pulp.

Heat the oil in a wok or a large saucepan and cook the beef in batches over high heat for 5 minutes, or until browned. Reduce the heat, add the coconut milk and cardamom, and simmer for 1 hour, or until the beef is tender. Remove the beef, strain and reserve the meat and also the cooking liquid separately.

Heat the coconut cream in the wok and stir in the curry paste. Cook for 5 minutes, or until the oil starts to separate from the cream.

Add the onions, potatoes, fish sauce, palm sugar, peanuts, beef mixture, reserved cooking liquid and tamarind water, and simmer for 25–30 minutes. Serve with coriander and rice.

note *Use small onions and potatoes, about 20–30 g (¾–1 oz) each.*

mexican beef stew

500 g (1 lb 2 oz) Roma tomatoes, halved
6 flour tortillas
1–2 red chillies, finely chopped
1 tablespoon olive oil
1 kg (2 lb 4 oz) stewing beef, cubed
½ teaspoon black pepper
2 onions, thinly sliced
375 ml (13 fl oz/1½ cups) beef stock
60 g (2 oz/¼ cup) tomato paste
   (concentrated purée)
375 g (13 oz) tin kidney beans, drained
1 teaspoon chilli powder
125 g (4½ oz/½ cup) sour cream
flat-leaf (Italian) parsley to garnish

serves 6

method Preheat the oven to 180°C (350°F/Gas 4). Grill (broil) the tomatoes, skin side up, under a hot grill (broiler) for 6–8 minutes, or until the skin is black and blistered. Place in a plastic bag and seal. Cool, remove the skin and roughly chop the flesh.

Bake two of the tortillas for 4 minutes, or until crisp. Break into pieces and put in a food processor with the tomato and chopped chilli. Process for 30 seconds, or until almost smooth.

Heat the oil in a large heavy-based saucepan. Brown the beef in batches, season with pepper, then remove. Add the onion to the pan and cook for 5 minutes. Return the meat to the pan. Stir in the processed mixture, stock and tomato paste, and bring to the boil. Reduce the heat, cover and simmer for 1¼ hours. Add the beans and chilli powder, and heat through.

Grill the remaining tortillas for 2–3 minutes on each side, then cool and cut into wedges. Serve the stew with the sour cream, and toasted tortilla wedges on the side.

hint *If this stew becomes too thick during cooking, thin it with a little extra stock.*

   100 EASY RECIPES ONE-POTS

veal goulash

500 g (1 lb 2 oz) veal, cut into 2.5 cm
(1 inch) pieces
2 tablespoons plain (all-purpose) flour
2 tablespoons olive oil
2 onions, thinly sliced
2 garlic cloves, finely chopped
1 tablespoon sweet paprika
1 teaspoon ground cumin
440 g (15½ oz) tin chopped tomatoes
2 carrots, sliced
½ red capsicum (pepper), chopped
½ green capsicum (pepper), chopped
250 ml (9 fl oz/1 cup) beef stock
125 ml (4 fl oz/½ cup) red wine
125 g (4½ oz/½ cup) sour cream
chopped flat-leaf (Italian) parsley, to garnish

serves 4

method Put the veal and flour in a plastic bag and shake to coat the veal with the flour. Shake off any excess. Heat 1 tablespoon of the oil in a large, deep heavy-based saucepan over medium heat. Brown the meat well in batches, then remove the meat and set aside.

Add the remaining oil to the pan. Cook the onion, garlic, paprika and cumin for 5 minutes, stirring frequently. Return the meat and any juices to the pan with the tomato, carrot and capsicum. Cover and cook for 10 minutes.

Add the stock and wine, and season with salt and pepper. Stir well, then cover and simmer over very low heat for 1½ hours. Stir in half the sour cream, season with more salt and pepper if needed and serve garnished with parsley and the remaining sour cream if desired. Delicious served with buttered boiled small potatoes or noodles.

note *If you prefer your sauce to be a little thicker, cook, uncovered, for 5 minutes over high heat before adding the sour cream.*

thai beef and peanut curry

method To make the curry paste, soak the chillies in boiling water for 5 minutes, or until soft. Remove the stem and seeds, then chop. Place all the curry paste ingredients in a food processor and process to a smooth paste. Add a little peanut oil if it is too thick.

Place the oil and the thick cream from the top of the coconut cream (reserving the rest) in a large saucepan over high heat. Add 6–8 tablespoons of the curry paste and cook, stirring, for 5 minutes, or until fragrant. Cook for 5–10 minutes, or until the coconut cream splits and becomes oily.

Add the beef, the reserved coconut cream, the coconut milk, makrut leaves and peanut butter, and cook for 8 minutes, or until the beef just starts to change colour. Reduce the heat and simmer for 1 hour, or until the beef is tender.

Stir in the lime juice, fish sauce and palm sugar, and transfer to a serving dish. Garnish with the Thai basil leaves, and extra peanuts, if desired, and serve immediately.

100 EASY RECIPES ONE-POTS

beef and red wine stew

30 g (1 oz) butter
2 tablespoons oil
1 kg (2 lb 4 oz) topside steak, trimmed and cut
into 3 cm (1¼ inch) cubes
100 g (3½ oz) bacon pieces, cut into 1.5 cm
(⅝ inch) cubes
18 baby onions
2 garlic cloves, crushed
30 g (1 oz/¼ cup) plain (all-purpose) flour
500 ml (17 fl oz/2 cups) red wine
750 ml (26 fl oz/3 cups) beef stock
300 g (10½ oz) small mushrooms, halved

serves 6

method   Heat the butter and oil in a heavy-based saucepan. Cook the meat quickly in small batches over medium–high heat until browned, then drain on paper towels.

Add the bacon, onions and garlic to the pan, and cook, stirring, for 2 minutes, or until browned. Add the flour and stir over low heat until lightly golden. Gradually pour in the wine and stock, and stir until smooth. Stir continuously over medium heat for 2 minutes, or until the mixture boils and thickens.

Return the meat to the pan and reduce the heat to a simmer. Cook, covered, for 1½ hours, or until the meat is tender, stirring occasionally. Add the mushrooms and cook for 15 minutes. Delicious served with mashed potato.

lamb

lamb hotpot

2 tablespoons olive oil
8 lamb shanks
2 onions, sliced
4 garlic cloves, finely chopped
3 bay leaves, torn in half
1–2 teaspoons hot paprika
2 teaspoons sweet paprika
1 tablespoon plain (all-purpose) flour
60 g (2 oz/¼ cup) tomato paste
   (concentrated purée)
1.5 litres (52 fl oz/6 cups) vegetable stock
4 potatoes, chopped
4 carrots, sliced
3 celery stalks, thickly sliced
3 tomatoes, seeded and chopped

serves 4

method To make the lamb stock, heat 1 tablespoon of the oil in a large heavy-based saucepan over medium heat. Brown the shanks well in two batches, then drain on paper towels.

Add the remaining oil to the pan and cook the onion, garlic and bay leaves over low heat for about 10 minutes, stirring regularly. Add the paprikas and flour and cook, stirring, for 2 minutes. Gradually add the combined tomato paste and vegetable stock. Bring to the boil, stirring continuously, and return the shanks to the pan. Reduce the heat to low and simmer, covered, for 1½ hours, stirring occasionally.

Remove and discard the bay leaves. Remove the shanks, allow to cool slightly and then cut the meat from the bone. Discard the bone. Cut the meat into pieces and refrigerate. Refrigerate for about 1 hour, or until fat forms on the surface and it can be spooned off.

Return the meat to the stock along with the potato, carrot and celery, turn the heat up to medium–high and bring to the boil. Reduce the heat and simmer for 15 minutes. Season with salt and pepper, and add the chopped tomato to serve.

mongolian lamb hotpot

250 g (9 oz) dried rice vermicelli
600 g (1 lb 5 oz) lamb backstraps, thinly sliced
across the grain
4 spring onions (scallions), sliced
1.5 litres (52 fl oz/6 cups) light chicken stock
3 cm x 6 cm (1¼ inch x 2½ inch) piece fresh
ginger, cut into 6 slices
2 tablespoons Chinese rice wine
300 g (10½ oz) silken firm tofu, cut into 1.5 cm
(⅝ inch) cubes
300 g (10½ oz) Chinese broccoli (gai larn), cut
into 4 cm (1½ inch) lengths
90 g (3 oz/2 cups) shredded Chinese
cabbage (wong bok)

sauce

80 ml (2½ fl oz/⅓ cup) light soy sauce
2 tablespoons Chinese sesame paste
1 tablespoon Chinese rice wine
1 teaspoon chilli and garlic paste

serves 6

method Place the vermicelli in a large heatproof bowl, cover with boiling water and soak for about 6 minutes. Drain well and divide among six serving bowls. Top with the lamb slices and spring onion.

To make the sauce, put the soy sauce, sesame paste, rice wine and the chilli and garlic paste in a small bowl and mix together.

Place the stock, ginger and rice wne in a 2.5 litre (87 fl oz/10 cup) flameproof hotpot or large saucepan. Cover and bring to the boil over high heat. Add the tofu, Chinese broccoli and Chinese cabbage and simmer, uncovered, for 1 minute, or until the cabbage has wilted. Divide the tofu, broccoli and cabbage among the serving bowls, then ladle on the hot stock. Drizzle a little of the sauce on top and serve the rest on the side.

lamb and bean casserole

300 g (10½ oz/1½ cups) borlotti (cranberry)
   beans or red kidney beans
1 kg (2 lb 4 oz) boned leg of lamb
1½ tablespoons olive oil
2 bacon slices, rind removed, chopped
1 large onion, chopped
2 garlic cloves, crushed
1 large carrot, chopped
500 ml (17 fl oz/2 cups) dry red wine
1 tablespoon tomato paste (concentrated
   purée)
375 ml (13 fl oz/1½ cups) beef stock
2 large rosemary sprigs
2 thyme sprigs
small thyme sprigs, extra, to garnish

serves 6

method Put the beans in a bowl and cover with plenty of water. Leave to soak overnight, then drain well.

Preheat the oven to 160°C (315°F/Gas 2–3). Trim any excess fat from the lamb and cut the lamb into 3 cm (1¼ inch) pieces.

Heat 1 tablespoon of the oil in a large flameproof casserole dish. Add half the meat and toss over medium–high heat for 2 minutes, or until browned. Remove from the dish and repeat with the remaining lamb. Remove from the dish.

Heat the remaining olive oil in the casserole dish and add the bacon and onion. Cook over medium heat for 3 minutes, or until the onion is translucent. Add the garlic and carrot, and cook for 1 minute, or until aromatic.

Return the meat and any juices to the casserole dish, increase the heat to high and add the wine. Bring to the boil and cook for 2 minutes. Add the beans, tomato paste, stock, rosemary sprigs and thyme sprigs, return to the boil, then cover, place in the oven and cook for 2 hours, or until the meat is tender. Stir occasionally during cooking. Skim off any excess fat, remove the sprigs of herbs. Season and garnish with extra thyme sprigs to serve.

lamb korma

2 kg (4 lb 8 oz) leg of lamb, boned
1 onion, chopped
2 teaspoons grated fresh ginger
3 garlic cloves
2 teaspoons ground coriander
2 teaspoons ground cumin
1 teaspoon cardamom seeds
large pinch cayenne pepper
2 tablespoons ghee or oil
1 onion, extra, sliced
2½ tablespoons tomato paste (concentrated purée)
125 g (4½ oz/½ cup) plain yoghurt
125 ml (4 fl oz/½ cup) coconut cream
55 g (2 oz/½ cup) ground almonds
toasted slivered almonds, to serve

serves 4–6

method Trim any excess fat or sinew from the lamb, cut it into 3 cm (1¼ inch) cubes and place in a large bowl.

Place the chopped onion, ginger, garlic, coriander, cumin, cardamom seeds, cayenne pepper and ½ teaspoon salt in a food processor. Process the ingredients until they form a smooth paste. Add the spice mixture to the cubed lamb and mix well to coat the lamb in the spices. Leave to marinate for 1 hour.

Heat the ghee in a large saucepan, add the sliced onion and cook, stirring, over low heat for about 7 minutes, or until the onion is soft. Add the lamb and spice mixture, and cook, stirring constantly, for 8–10 minutes, or until the lamb changes colour. Stir in the tomato paste, yoghurt, coconut cream and ground almonds.

Reduce the heat and simmer the curry, covered, stirring occasionally, for 50 minutes, or until the meat is tender. Add a little water if the mixture becomes too dry. Season the curry with salt and pepper, and garnish with the toasted slivered almonds. Serve with steamed rice.

lamb meatballs

1 kg (2 lb 4 oz) minced (ground) lamb
1 onion, finely chopped
2 garlic cloves, finely chopped
2 tablespoons finely chopped flat-leaf (Italian)
    parsley
2 tablespoons finely chopped coriander
    (cilantro) leaves
½ teaspoon cayenne pepper
½ teaspoon ground allspice
½ teaspoon ground ginger
½ teaspoon ground cardamom
1 teaspoon ground cumin
1 teaspoon paprika

sauce

2 tablespoons olive oil
1 onion, finely chopped
2 garlic cloves, finely chopped
2 teaspoons ground cumin
½ teaspoon ground cinnamon
1 teaspoon paprika
2 x 400 g (14 oz) tins chopped tomatoes
2 teaspoons harissa
1 bunch coriander (cilantro) leaves, chopped

serves 4

method Preheat the oven to 180°C (350°F/Gas 4). Lightly grease two baking trays. Place the lamb, onion, garlic, herbs and spices in a bowl, and mix together well and then season. Roll tablespoons of the mixture into balls and place on trays. Bake for 18–20 minutes, or until browned.

Meanwhile, to make the sauce, heat the oil in a large saucepan, add the onion and cook over medium heat for 5 minutes, or until soft. Add the garlic, cumin, cinnamon and paprika, and cook for 1 minute, or until fragrant.

Stir in the tomato and harissa, and bring to the boil. Reduce heat and simmer for 20 minutes, then add the meatballs and simmer for another 10 minutes, or until cooked. Stir in the coriander, and serve.

lamb's liver and bacon stew

1 lamb's liver, about 750 g (1 lb 10 oz)
(see Note)
30 g (1 oz/¼ cup) cornflour (cornstarch)
¼ teaspoon ground black pepper
6 bacon slices, cut into large pieces
2 tablespoons oil
2 onions, thinly sliced
1 beef stock (bouillon) cube, crumbled

serves 6

method Wash the liver and cut it into thin slices, discarding any veins or discoloured spots. Pat the liver dry with paper towels. Combine the cornflour and pepper. Toss the liver slices in the seasoned cornflour, shaking off the excess.

Cook the bacon in a heavy-based saucepan until crisp, then drain on paper towels. Heat the oil in the pan and cook the onion gently until golden, then remove from the pan.

Cook the liver quickly in small batches over medium heat until well browned, then drain on paper towels. Return the liver, bacon and onion to the pan. Dissolve the stock cube in 250 ml (9 fl oz/1 cup) boiling water, then gradually add to the pan. Stir over medium heat for 10 minutes, or until the liquid boils and thickens. Sprinkle with cracked black pepper and serve immediately.

note *Soaking the liver in milk for 30 minutes before cooking will result in a milder taste.*

lamb tagine

1.5 kg (3 lb 5 oz) leg or shoulder of lamb, cut
   into 2.5 cm (1 inch) pieces
3 garlic cloves, chopped
80 ml (2½ fl oz/⅓ cup) olive oil
2 teaspoons ground cumin
1 teaspoon ground ginger
1 teaspoon ground turmeric
1 teaspoon paprika
½ teaspoon ground cinnamon
2 onions, thinly sliced
600 ml (21 fl oz) beef stock
¼ preserved lemon, pulp discarded, zest rinsed
   and cut into thin strips
425 g (15 oz) tin chickpeas, drained
35 g (1 oz) cracked green olives (see Note)
1 large handful chopped coriander (cilantro)
   leaves, plus extra to garnish

serves 6–8

method Place the lamb pieces in a non-metallic bowl, add the garlic, 2 tablespoons of the oil and the ground cumin, ginger, turmeric, paprika, cinnamon, and ½ teaspoon ground black pepper and 1 teaspoon salt. Mix well to coat, then leave to marinate for 1 hour.

Heat the remaining oil in a large saucepan, add the lamb in batches and cook over high heat for 2–3 minutes, or until browned. Remove from the pan. Add the onion and cook for 2 minutes, then return the meat to the pan and add the beef stock. Reduce the heat and simmer, covered, for 1 hour.

Add the preserved lemon strips, drained chickpeas and olives, and cook, uncovered, for a further 30 minutes, or until the lamb is tender and the sauce has reduced and thickened. Stir in the coriander. Serve in bowls and garnish with extra coriander.

note *Cracked green olives are marinated in herbs and are available from specialty shops.*

100 EASY RECIPES ONE-POTS

lamb shanks in tomato sauce on polenta

2 tablespoons olive oil
1 large red onion, sliced
4 French-trimmed lamb shanks
(about 250 g/9 oz each) (see Note)
2 garlic cloves, crushed
400 g (14 oz) tin chopped tomatoes
125 ml (4 fl oz/½ cup) red wine
2 teaspoons chopped rosemary
150 g (5½ oz/1 cup) instant polenta
50 g (2 oz) butter
50 g (2 oz/½ cup) grated parmesan cheese
rosemary, extra, to garnish

serves 4

method Preheat the oven to 160°C (315°F/Gas 2–3). Heat the oil in a 4 litre (140 fl oz/16 cup) flameproof casserole dish over medium heat and sauté the onion for 3–4 minutes, or until softening and becoming transparent. Add the lamb shanks and cook for 2–3 minutes, or until lightly browned. Add the garlic, tomato and wine, then bring to the boil and cook for 3–4 minutes. Stir in the rosemary. Season with ¼ teaspoon each of salt and pepper.

Cover and bake for 2 hours. Remove the lid, return to the oven and simmer for a further 15 minutes, or until the lamb just starts to fall off the bone. Check periodically that the sauce is not too dry, adding water if needed.

About 20 minutes before serving, bring 1 litre (35 fl oz/4 cups) water to the boil in a saucepan. Add the polenta in a thin stream, whisking continuously, then reduce the heat to very low. Simmer for 8–10 minutes, or until thick and coming away from the side of pan. Stir in the butter and parmesan. To serve, spoon the polenta onto serving plates, top with the shanks and tomato sauce. Top with rosemary.

note *French-trimmed lamb shanks are lamb shanks with the meat scraped back to make a neat lamb 'drumstick'. If these are unavailable, you can use regular lamb shanks instead.*

lamb rogan josh

1 tablespoon ghee or oil
2 onions, chopped
125 g (4½ oz/½ cup) plain yoghurt
1 teaspoon chilli powder
1 tablespoon ground coriander
2 teaspoons ground cumin
1 teaspoon ground cardamom
½ teaspoon ground cloves
1 teaspoon ground turmeric
3 garlic cloves, crushed
1 tablespoon grated fresh ginger
400 g (14 oz) tin chopped tomatoes
1 kg (2 lb 4 oz) boned leg of lamb, cut into
  2.5 cm (1 inch) cubes
30 g (1 oz/¼ cup) slivered almonds
1 teaspoon garam masala
coriander (cilantro) leaves, to garnish

serves 4–6

method Heat the ghee in a large saucepan, add the onion and cook, stirring, for 5 minutes, or until soft. Stir in the yoghurt, chilli powder, coriander, cumin, cardamom, cloves, turmeric, garlic and ginger. Add the tomato and 1 teaspoon salt, and simmer for 5 minutes.

Add the lamb and stir until coated. Cover and cook over low heat, stirring occasionally, for 1–1½ hours, or until the lamb is tender. Uncover and simmer until the liquid thickens.

Meanwhile, toast the almonds in a dry frying pan over medium heat for 3–4 minutes, shaking the pan gently, until the nuts are golden brown. Remove from the pan at once to prevent them from burning.

Add the garam masala to the curry and mix through well. Sprinkle the slivered almonds and coriander leaves over the top. Serve with steamed rice and chapattis.

100 EASY RECIPES ONE-POTS

navarin of lamb

8 lamb noisettes (see Notes)
seasoned plain (all-purpose) flour
2 tablespoons oil
2 celery stalks, sliced thinly
12 baby carrots, peeled (see Notes)
12 new potatoes, halved
6 thyme sprigs
1 large handful flat-leaf (Italian) parsley, chopped
2 onions, chopped
2 garlic cloves, crushed
40 g (1½ oz/⅓ cup) plain (all-purpose) flour
625 ml (21½ fl oz/2½ cups) chicken stock
250 ml (9 fl oz/1 cup) red wine
60 g (2 oz/¼ cup) tomato paste (concentrated purée)
chopped flat-leaf (Italian) parsley, extra, to garnish

serves 4

method Toss the lamb in the seasoned flour, shaking off the excess. Preheat the oven to 180°C (350°F/Gas 4).

Heat the oil in a heavy-based saucepan. In batches, brown the lamb well on both sides over medium–high heat. Remove the lamb from the heat, drain well on paper towels, then transfer to a greased, 3 litre (105 fl oz/12 cup) casserole dish. Top with the celery, carrots, potatoes, thyme sprigs and parsley.

Cook the onion and garlic in the same saucepan, stirring over medium heat for 5–10 minutes, or until the onion is soft.

Add the flour and stir for 1 minute, or until the onion is coated. Add the stock, wine and tomato paste and stir until the sauce boils and thickens. Pour the sauce over the lamb and vegetables. Bake, covered, for 1¼ hours, or until the lamb is tender. Carefully remove the string from the lamb, and sprinkle with extra parsley to serve.

notes *A noisette is a round slice of meat, cut from a boned loin and tied with string to hold its shape. For this recipe you could also use a boned leg of lamb, cut into 3 cm (1¼ inch) cubes. If baby carrots are not available, use four sliced carrots instead.*

pork

pasta and bean soup

200 g (7 oz) dried borlotti (cranberry) beans (see Note)
60 ml (2 fl oz/¼ cup) olive oil
90 g (3 oz) piece pancetta, finely diced
1 onion, finely chopped
2 garlic cloves, crushed
1 celery stalk, thinly sliced
1 carrot, diced
1 bay leaf
1 rosemary sprig
1 flat-leaf (Italian) parsley sprig
400 g (14 oz) tin chopped tomatoes, drained
1.6 litres (56 fl oz) vegetable stock
2 tablespoons finely chopped flat-leaf (Italian) parsley
150 g (5½ oz) ditalini or other small dried pasta
extra virgin olive oil, to serve
grated parmesan cheese, to serve

serves 4

method Place the beans in a large bowl, cover with cold water and soak overnight. Drain and rinse.

Heat the oil in a large saucepan, add the pancetta, onion, garlic, celery and carrot, and cook over medium heat for 5 minutes, or until golden. Season. Add the bay leaf, rosemary, parsley sprig, tomato, stock and beans. Bring to the boil. Reduce heat and simmer for 1½ hours, or until tender. Add boiling water if needed.

Discard the bay leaf, rosemary and parsley sprigs. Scoop out 250 ml (9 fl oz/1 cup) of the mixture and purée in a food processor. Return to the pan, season, and add chopped parsley and pasta. Simmer for 6 minutes, or until al dente. Remove from heat and set aside for 10 minutes. Serve drizzled with olive oil, sprinkled with parmesan and pepper if desired.

note *If you prefer, you can use three 400 g (14 oz) tins drained borlotti beans. Simmer with the other vegetables for 30 minutes.*

100 EASY RECIPES ONE-POTS

eight-treasure noodle soup

10 g (¼ oz) dried shiitake mushrooms
375 g (13 oz) fresh thick hokkein (egg) noodles
1.2 litres (42 fl oz/5 cups) chicken stock
60 ml (2 fl oz/¼ cup) light soy sauce
2 teaspoons Chinese rice wine
200 g (7 oz) boneless, skinless chicken breasts,
cut into 1 cm (½ inch) strips on the diagonal
200 g (7 oz) Chinese barbecued pork (char siu),
cut into 5 mm (¼ inch) slices
¼ onion, finely chopped
1 carrot, cut into 1 cm (½ inch) sliced on the
diagonal
120 g (4 oz) snow peas (mangetout), cut in
half on the diagonal
4 bulb spring onions (scallions), thinly sliced

serves 4

method Soak the mushrooms in boiling water for 20 minutes, or until soft. Drain and squeeze out any excess liquid. Discard the stems and thinly slice the caps.

Bring a large saucepan of water to the boil and cook the noodles for 1 minute, or until cooked through. Drain, then rinse with cold water. Divide evenly among four deep warmed serving bowls.

Meanwhile, bring the chicken stock to the boil in a large saucepan over high heat. Reduce the heat to medium and stir in the soy sauce and rice wine. Simmer for 2 minutes. Add the chicken and pork and cook for 2 minutes, or until the chicken is cooked and the pork is heated through. Add the onion, carrot, snow peas, mushrooms and half the spring onion, and cook for 1 minute, or until the carrot is tender.

Divide the vegetables and meat among the serving bowls and ladle on the hot broth. Garnish with the remaining spring onion.

pork and coriander stew

1 ½ tablespoons coriander seeds
800 g (1 lb 12 oz) pork fillet, cut into 2 cm
   (¾ inch) cubes
1 tablespoon plain (all-purpose) flour
60 ml (2 fl oz/¼ cup) olive oil
1 large onion, thinly sliced
375 ml (13 fl oz/1 ½ cups) red wine
250 ml (9 fl oz/1 cup) chicken stock
1 teaspoon sugar
fresh coriander (cilantro) sprigs, to garnish

serves 4–6

method Crush the coriander seeds in a mortar with a pestle. Combine the pork, seeds and ½ teaspoon cracked pepper. Cover and marinate overnight in the refrigerator.

Combine the flour and pork, and toss to coat. Heat 2 tablespoons of the oil in a saucepan and cook the pork in batches over high heat. Remove.

Heat the remaining oil, add the onion and cook over medium heat for 2–3 minutes, or until golden. Return the meat to the pan, add the wine, stock and sugar. Season. Bring to the boil, then reduce the heat and simmer, covered, for 1 hour.

Remove the meat. Return the pan to the heat and boil over high heat for 3–5 minutes, or until the liquid reduces and thickens. Pour over the meat and garnish with coriander. Serve with boiled potatoes.

ham, leek and potato ragu

50 g (2 oz) butter
2 tablespoons olive oil
250 g (9 oz) piece double-smoked ham, cut
into cubes (see Note)
3 garlic cloves, finely chopped
3 leeks (white part only), sliced
1.5 kg (3 lb 5 oz) potatoes, peeled and cut into
large chunks
500 ml (17 fl oz/2 cups) chicken stock
2 tablespoons brandy
125 ml (4 fl oz/½ cup) cream
1 tablespoon each of chopped oregano and
parsley

serves 4–6

method Heat the butter and oil in a large heavy-based saucepan. Cook the ham, garlic and leek over low heat for 10 minutes, stirring regularly. Add the potato and cook for 10 minutes, stirring regularly.

Slowly stir in the stock and brandy. Cover and gently simmer. Cook for another 15–20 minutes until the potato is tender but still chunky, and sauce has thickened. Add cream and herbs, and season. Simmer for another 5 minutes.

note *You can use any type of ham for this recipe. A double-smoked ham will give a good, hearty flavour.*

pork and eggplant hotpot

olive oil, for cooking
375 g (13 oz) slender eggplants (aubergines),
   cut into 3 cm (1¼ inch) slices
8 bulb spring onions (scallions)
400 g (14 oz) tin chopped tomatoes
2 garlic cloves, crushed
2 teaspoons ground cumin
500 g (1 lb 2 oz) pork fillet, cut into 3 cm
   (1¼ inch) thick slices
seasoned plain (all-purpose) flour
170 ml (5½ fl oz/⅔ cup) cider
1 rosemary sprig
2 tablespoons chopped toasted almonds

serves 4

method   Heat 60 ml (2 fl oz/¼ cup) of oil in a large heavy-based frying pan. Brown the eggplant in batches over high heat, adding oil as needed. Remove and set aside.

Quarter the spring onions along their length. Add some oil to the pan and fry the spring onion over medium heat for 5 minutes. Add the tomato, garlic and cumin, and cook for 2 minutes. Remove from the pan and set aside.

Coat the pork in the seasoned flour, shaking off any excess. Brown in batches over medium–high heat until golden, adding oil as needed. Remove and set aside.

Add the cider to the pan and stir well, scraping down the side and base. Allow to boil for 1–2 minutes, then add 125 ml (4 fl oz/½ cup) water. Reduce the heat and stir in the spring onion and tomato mixture. Add the pork, season, and poke the rosemary sprig into the stew. Partially cover and simmer gently for 20 minutes.

Layer the eggplant on top, partially cover and cook for 25 minutes, or until the pork is tender. Just before serving, gently toss the almonds through.

caramel pork with shanghai noodles

500 g (1 lb 2 oz) Shanghai noodles
700 g (1 lb 9 oz) boneless pork belly
2 teaspoons peanut oil
150 g (5½ oz) caster (superfine) sugar
5 garlic cloves, crushed
5 slices fresh ginger, 5 mm (¼ inch) thick
2 lemongrass stems (white part only), bruised
1 teaspoon white pepper
500 ml (17 fl oz/2 cups) chicken stock
70 ml (3 fl oz) fish sauce
100 g (3½ oz) tinned bamboo shoots,
drained well
4 spring onions (scallions), cut into 3 cm
(1¼ inch) pieces
1 tablespoon lime juice
1 tablespoon chopped coriander (cilantro)
leaves (optional)
1 bunch bok choy (pak choy), (optional)

serves 4

method Cook the Shanghai noodles in a large saucepan of boiling water for 4–5 minutes, or until tender. Rinse, drain and cut the noodles into 10 cm (4 inch) lengths.

Preheat the oven to 180°C (350°F/Gas 4). Cut the pork belly across the grain into 1 cm (½ inch) thick slices, then cut each slice into 2 cm (¾ inch) pieces. Heat the oil in a 4 litre (140 fl oz/16 cup) flameproof casserole dish over medium–high heat. Cook the pork in two batches for 5 minutes, or until it starts to brown all over. Remove the pork and drain off the fat.

Add the sugar and 2 tablespoons water to the casserole dish, stirring until the sugar has dissolved and scraping up any sediment that may have stuck to the bottom. Increase heat to high and cook for 2–3 minutes without stirring until dark golden, being careful not to burn—you should just be able to smell the caramel.

Return the pork to the casserole dish, then stir in the garlic, ginger, lemongrass, white pepper, stock, 2 tablespoons of the fish sauce and 375 ml (12 fl oz/1½ cups) water. Place the dish in the oven and bake, covered, for 1 hour, then remove the lid and cook for a further 1 hour, or until the pork is very tender. Carefully remove the ginger and the lemongrass stems.

Add the noodles to the casserole dish with the bamboo shoots, spring onion, lime juice and remaining fish sauce, and stir to combine. Return the dish to the oven for a further 10 minutes to heat through. Stir in the coriander, if desired, and serve with steamed bok choy and steamed Asian greens, if desired.

pork ball curry with egg noodles

200 g (7 oz) minced (ground) pork
3 garlic cloves, chopped
2 lemongrass stems, white part only, finely
   chopped
2.5 cm (1 inch) piece ginger, grated
1 tablespoon oil
1–2 tablespoons green curry paste, to taste
375 ml (13 fl oz/1½ cups) coconut milk
2 tablespoons fish sauce
2 teaspoons soft brown sugar
1 medium handful chopped Thai basil leaves
200 g (7 oz) fresh egg noodles
sliced spring onions (scallions), coriander
   (cilantro) leaves and sliced chillies, to serve

serves 4

method Finely chop the minced pork with a cleaver or large knife. Combine the pork, garlic, lemongrass and ginger in a bowl and mix thoroughly. Form teaspoonfuls into small balls.

Heat the oil in a wok, add the curry paste and cook over low heat, stirring constantly, for 1 minute, or until fragrant. Add the coconut milk and 250 ml (9 fl oz/1 cup) water to the wok. Stir until boiling, then reduce the heat and simmer for 5 minutes. Add the pork balls and simmer for 5 minutes, or until cooked. Add the fish sauce, brown sugar and Thai basil.

Cook the noodles in boiling water for 4 minutes, or until tender, then drain. Toss with the pork balls and curry sauce and then serve immediately, as the noodles will soak up the sauce. Scatter spring onions, coriander and chillies over the top.

italian sausage and chickpea stew

2 large red capsicums (peppers)
1 tablespoon olive oil
2 large red onions, cut into thick wedges
2 garlic cloves, finely chopped
600 g (1 lb 5 oz) Italian-style thin pork sausages
300 g (10½ oz) chickpeas, drained
150 g (5½ oz) flat mushrooms, thickly sliced
125 ml (4 fl oz/½ cup) dry white wine
2 bay leaves
2 teaspoons chopped rosemary
400 g (14 oz) tin chopped tomatoes

serves 4

method Cut the capsicums into large pieces, removing the seeds and membrane. Place skin side up, under a hot grill (broiler) until the skin blackens and blisters. Allow to cool in a sealed plastic bag. Peel away the skin, and slice diagonally into thick strips.

Meanwhile, heat the oil in a large non-stick frying pan. Add the onion and garlic, and stir over medium heat for 6 minutes, or until the onion is soft and browned. Remove the onion from the pan and set aside. Add the sausages to the same pan. Cook over medium heat, turning occasionally, for 8 minutes, or until the sausages are browned. Remove the sausages from the pan, allow to cool and slice diagonally into 3 cm (1¼ inch) pieces.

Combine the capsicum slices, onion, sausage pieces, chickpeas and mushrooms in the frying pan, and cook over medium–high heat.

Add the wine, bay leaves and rosemary to the pan. Bring to the boil, then reduce the heat to low and simmer for 3 minutes. Stir in the tomato and simmer for 20 minutes, or until the sauce has thickened slightly. Remove the bay leaves and season to taste with sugar, salt and cracked black pepper. Delicious served with fettuccine, grilled ciabatta bread, mashed potato, soft polenta or parmesan cheese shavings.

braised pork with prunes

4 lean pork loin medallions, about 175 g
  (6 oz) each
500 ml (17 fl oz/2 cups) chicken stock
2 tablespoons oil
1 large onion, cut into wedges
2 garlic cloves, crushed
1 tablespoon thyme leaves
1 large tomato, peeled, seeded and finely
  chopped
125 ml (4 fl oz/½ cup) cream
16 pitted prunes

serves 4

method Shape the meat into rounds by tying a length of string around the medallions. Tie with a bow for easy removal. Bring the stock to the boil in a medium saucepan. Reduce the heat to a simmer and cook for 5 minutes, or until reduced to 185 ml (6 fl oz/¾ cup).

Heat the oil over high heat in a heavy-based frying pan. Cook the meat for 2 minutes each side to seal, turning once. Drain on paper towels.

Add the onion and garlic to the frying pan, and stir for 2 minutes. Return the meat to the pan with the thyme, tomato and stock, then reduce the heat to low. Cover the pan and bring slowly to simmering point. Simmer for 10 minutes, or until the meat is tender, turning once. Add the cream and prunes, and simmer for a further 5 minutes. Remove the string and serve with greens.

100 EASY RECIPES ONE-POTS

pork and tamarind curry

80 ml (2½ fl oz/⅓ cup) oil
2 onions, thickly sliced
4 large garlic cloves, crushed
30 g (1 oz/¼ cup) Sri Lankan curry powder
1 tablespoon grated fresh ginger
10 dried curry leaves or 5 fresh curry leaves
2 teaspoons chilli powder
¼ teaspoon fenugreek seeds
1.25 kg (2 lb 12 oz) lean pork shoulder, cubed
1 lemongrass stem (white part only), finely
chopped
2 tablespoons tamarind purée
4 cardamom pods, crushed
400 ml (14 fl oz) tin coconut cream

cucumber sambal

1–2 large cucumbers, halved, seeded and finely
chopped
500 g (1 lb 2 oz/2 cups) plain yoghurt
2 tablespoons coriander (cilantro) leaves, finely
chopped
1 tablespoon lemon juice
2 garlic cloves, crushed

serves 6

method Heat the oil in a heavy-based Dutch oven or deep, lidded frying pan. Add the onion, garlic, curry powder, ginger, curry leaves, chilli powder, fenugreek seeds and 1 teaspoon salt, and cook, stirring, over medium heat for 5 minutes.

Add the pork, lemongrass, tamarind purée, cardamom and 375 ml (13 fl oz/1½ cups) hot water, then reduce the heat and simmer, covered, for 1 hour.

Stir in the coconut cream and simmer on a low heat, uncovered, for 40–45 minutes, or until the sauce has reduced and become thick and creamy.

To make the cucumber sambal, place the cucumber in a bowl and stir in the yoghurt, coriander, lemon juice and garlic. Season to taste with salt and pepper.

Serve the curry with the cucumber sambal, steamed basmati rice and chapattis.

pork, beer and chickpea stew

2 teaspoons ground cumin
1 teaspoon ground coriander
½ teaspoon chilli powder
¼ teaspoon ground cinnamon
400 g (14 oz) lean diced pork, trimmed
1 tablespoon plain (all-purpose) flour
1 tablespoon olive oil
1 large onion, finely chopped
3 garlic cloves, finely chopped
2 large carrots, finely chopped
2 celery stalks, thinly sliced
125 ml (4 fl oz/½ cup) chicken stock
125 ml (4 fl oz/½ cup) beer
2 ripe tomatoes, chopped
310 g (11 oz) tin chickpeas, rinsed
2 tablespoons chopped parsley

serves 4

method Cook the spices in a dry frying pan over low heat, shaking the pan, for 1 minute, or until aromatic.

Combine the pork with the spices and flour in a plastic bag and toss well. Remove the pork and shake off the excess flour. Heat the oil in a large heavy-based saucepan over high heat and cook the pork, tossing regularly, for 8 minutes, or until lightly browned.

Add the onion, garlic, carrot, celery and half the stock to the pan and toss well. Cover and cook for 10 minutes. Add the remaining stock, beer and tomato and season to taste. Bring to the boil, reduce the heat, cover with a tight-fitting lid, then simmer over low heat for 1 hour. Gently shake the pan occasionally, but do not remove the lid during cooking. Stir in the chickpeas and parsley. Simmer, uncovered, for 5 minutes and serve.

100 EASY RECIPES ONE-POTS

pork sausage and white bean stew

350 g (12 oz) dried white haricot beans
150 g (5½ oz) tocino, speck or pancetta, unsliced
½ leek (white part only), thinly sliced
2 garlic cloves
1 bay leaf
1 small red chilli, halved and seeded
1 small onion
2 cloves
1 rosemary sprig
3 thyme sprigs
1 parsley sprig
60 ml (2 fl oz/¼ cup) olive oil
8 pork sausages
½ onion, finely chopped
1 green capsicum (pepper), finely chopped
½ teaspoon paprika
125 g (4½ oz/½ cup) tomato paste (concentrated purée)
1 teaspoon cider vinegar

serves 4

method Soak the beans overnight in cold water. Drain and rinse the beans under cold water. Put them in a large saucepan with the tocino, leek, garlic, bay leaf and chilli. Stud the onion with the cloves and add to the saucepan. Tie the rosemary, thyme and parsley together, and add to the saucepan. Pour in 750 ml (26 fl oz/3 cups) cold water and bring to the boil. Add 1 tablespoon of the oil, reduce the heat and simmer, covered, for about 1 hour, or until the beans are tender. When necessary, add a little more boiling water to keep the beans covered.

Prick each sausage five or six times and twist tightly in opposite directions in the middle to give two short fat sausages joined in the middle. Put in a single layer in a large frying pan and add enough cold water to reach halfway up their sides. Bring to the boil and simmer, turning two or three times, until all the water has evaporated and the sausages brown lightly in the little fat that is left in the pan. Remove from the pan and cut the short sausages apart. Add the remaining oil, the chopped onion and capsicum to the pan, and fry over medium heat for 5–6 minutes. Stir in the paprika, cook for 30 seconds, then add the tomato paste. Season to taste. Cook, stirring, for 1 minute.

Remove the tocino, herb sprigs and any loose large pieces of onion from the bean mixture. Leave in any loose leaves from the herbs and any small pieces of onion. Add the sausages and sauce to the pan, and stir the vinegar through. Bring to the boil. Adjust the seasoning and serve.

seafood

prawn laksa

1 kg (2 lb 4 oz) raw prawns (shrimp)
80 ml (2½ fl oz/⅓ cup) oil
2–6 small red chillies, seeded
1 onion, roughly chopped
3 garlic cloves, halved
2 cm x 2 cm (¾ inch x ¾ inch) piece fresh
   ginger or galangal, chopped
3 lemongrass stems (white part only), chopped
1 teaspoon ground turmeric
1 tablespoon ground coriander
2 teaspoons shrimp paste
625 ml (21½ fl oz/2½ cups) coconut cream
2 teaspoons grated palm sugar (jaggery) or
   soft brown sugar
4 makrut (kaffir lime) leaves, crushed
1–2 tablespoons fish sauce
200 g (7 oz) packet fish balls
190 g (7 oz) fried tofu puffs
250 g (9 oz) dried rice vermicelli
125 g (4½ oz) bean sprouts, trimmed
1 large handful mint leaves, to serve
coriander (cilantro) leaves, to serve

serves 4

method Heat 2 tablespoons of the oil in a wok or large saucepan and add the prawn shells, tails and heads. Stir over medium heat for 10 minutes, or until orange, then add 1 litre (35 fl oz/4 cups) water. Bring to the boil, then reduce the heat and simmer for 15 minutes. Strain the stock through a fine sieve and reserve the liquid. Discard the shells and clean the pan.

Finely chop the chillies (use two for mild flavour, increase for hot), and process with the onion, garlic, ginger, lemongrass, turmeric, coriander and 60 ml (2 fl oz/¼ cup) of the prawn stock in a food processor.

Heat the remaining oil in the pan, add the chilli mixture and shrimp paste, and stir over medium heat for 3 minutes, or until fragrant. Pour in the remaining stock and simmer for 10 minutes. Add the coconut cream, palm sugar, makrut leaves and fish sauce, and simmer for 5 minutes. Add the prawns and simmer for 2 minutes, or until firm and light pink. Add the fish balls and fried tofu puffs, and simmer gently until just heated through.

Soak the rice vermicelli in a bowl of boiling water for 2 minutes, then drain and divide among serving bowls. Top with the bean sprouts and ladle the soup over the top. Garnish with the mint and coriander.

clam chowder

30 g (1 oz) butter
2 bacon slices, finely chopped
1 large onion, finely chopped
4 potatoes, cut into small cubes
500 ml (17 fl oz/2 cups) fish stock
1 bay leaf
125 ml (4 fl oz/½ cup) full-cream (whole) milk
4 x 105 g (3½ oz) tins baby clams (vongole),
drained and chopped
2 tablespoons finely chopped parsley
250 ml (9 fl oz/1 cup) cream
parsley, extra, to garnish

serves 4

method Heat the butter in a large saucepan. Cook the bacon and onion for 2–3 minutes, or until softened. Stir in the potato. Cook for a further 2–3 minutes, then gradually pour the stock into the pan. Add the bay leaf.

Bring the mixture to the boil, then reduce the heat and simmer, covered, for 20 minutes, or until the potato is cooked. Simmer for 10 minutes, or until the soup is reduced and slightly thickened. Discard the bay leaf.

Add the milk, clams, parsley and cream. Stir to gently reheat, but do not allow the soup to boil. Season with salt and freshly ground black pepper. Sprinkle with parsley to serve.

vietnamese fish and noodle soup

1 teaspoon shrimp paste
150 g (5½ oz) mung bean vermicelli
2 tablespoons peanut oil
6 garlic cloves, finely chopped
1 small onion, thinly sliced
2 long red chillies, chopped
2 lemongrass stems (white part only), thinly
　　sliced
1.25 litres (44 fl oz/5 cups) chicken stock
60 ml (2 fl oz/¼ cup) fish sauce
1 tablespoon rice vinegar
4 ripe tomatoes, peeled, seeded and chopped
500 g (1 lb 2 oz) firm white fish fillets (snapper
　　or blue-eyed cod), cut into 3 cm (1¼ inch)
　　pieces
1 large handful mint, torn
1 very large handful coriander (cilantro) leaves
90 g (3 oz/1 cup) bean sprouts, trimmed
1 tablespoon mint, extra
1 tablespoon coriander (cilantro) leaves, extra
2 long red chillies, extra, sliced
lemon wedges, to serve

serves 4

method Wrap the shrimp paste in foil and place under a hot grill (broiler) for 1 minute. Set aside.

Soak the vermicelli in boiling water for 3–4 minutes. Rinse under cold water, drain and then cut into 15 cm (6 inch) lengths.

Heat the oil in a heavy-based saucepan over medium heat. Add the garlic and cook for 1 minute, or until golden. Add the onion, chilli, lemongrass and paste, and cook, stirring, for a further minute. Add the stock, fish sauce, vinegar and tomato. Bring to the boil, then reduce the heat to medium and simmer for 10 minutes. Add the fish and simmer gently for 3 minutes, or until cooked. Stir in the mint and coriander.

Divide noodles and sprouts among bowls and ladle the soup on top. Top with extra mint, coriander and chilli. Serve with lemon wedges.

100 EASY RECIPES ONE-POTS

crab curry

4 raw large blue swimmer or mud crabs
1 tablespoon oil
1 large onion, finely chopped
2 garlic cloves, crushed
1 lemongrass stem (white part only), finely chopped
1 teaspoon sambal oelek (South-East Asian chilli paste)
1 teaspoon ground cumin
1 teaspoon ground turmeric
1 teaspoon ground coriander
270 ml (9½ fl oz) coconut cream
500 ml (17 fl oz/2 cups) chicken stock
1 large handful basil leaves

serves 6

method Pull back the apron and remove the top shell from the crabs. Remove the intestines and grey feathery gills. Cut each crab into four pieces. Use a cracker to crack the claws open; this will make it easier to eat later and will also allow the flavours to get into the crabmeat.

Heat the oil in a large saucepan or wok. Add the onion, garlic, lemongrass and sambal oelek, and cook for 2–3 minutes, or until softened. Add the cumin, turmeric, coriander and ½ teaspoon salt, and cook for a further 2 minutes, or until fragrant.

Stir in the coconut cream and stock. Bring to the boil, then reduce the heat, add the crab pieces and cook, stirring occasionally, for 10 minutes, or until the liquid has reduced and thickened slightly and the crabs are cooked. Scatter the basil leaves over the crab and serve with rice.

moroccan seafood with coriander

2 tablespoons olive oil
2 red onions, roughly chopped
1 red capsicum (pepper), chopped
4 garlic cloves, crushed
2 teaspoons ground cumin
1 teaspoon ground coriander
2 teaspoons sweet paprika
½ teaspoon dried chilli flakes
250 ml (9 fl oz/1 cup) chicken or fish stock
425 g (15 oz) tin chopped tomatoes
80 ml (2½ fl oz/⅓ cup) orange juice
1 tablespoon sugar
40 g (1½ oz/⅓ cup) raisins
375 g (13 oz) baby new potatoes
500 g (1 lb 2 oz) baby octopus, cleaned
12 raw king prawns (shrimp), peeled and
   deveined, leaving the tails intact
1 kg (2 lb 4 oz) thick white fish fillets, cut into
   chunks

coriander purée

2 very large handfuls coriander (cilantro) leaves
2 tablespoons ground almonds
80 ml (2½ fl oz/⅓ cup) extra virgin olive oil
½ teaspoon ground cumin
1 teaspoon honey

serves 6

method Heat the olive oil in a large saucepan and then cook the onion over medium heat for about 5 minutes, or until soft. Add the capsicum and garlic, and cook for another minute. Add the cumin, coriander, paprika and chilli flakes, and cook until fragrant.

Pour in the stock, tomato, orange juice, sugar and raisins, and bring to the boil. Add the potatoes, reduce the heat to low and gently simmer for 20–30 minutes, or until the potatoes are just tender. Season to taste.

Use a small sharp knife to remove the octopus heads; slit the heads open and remove the gut. Grasp the body firmly and push the beak out with your index finger; remove and discard. Add the octopus, prawns and fish to the pan and cook, covered, for 10 minutes, or until the fish flakes when tested with a fork.

To make the coriander purée, place the coriander leaves and ground almonds in a food processor. With the motor running, drizzle in the oil and process until smooth, then add the cumin, honey and salt to taste. Process until well combined.

To serve, dish the stew onto serving plates and drizzle a spoonful of purée on top. Serve with couscous and a green leaf salad.

100 EASY RECIPES ONE-POTS

seafood and fennel stew

2 tablespoons olive oil
1 large fennel bulb, thinly sliced
2 leeks (white part only), thinly sliced
2 garlic cloves, crushed
½ teaspoon paprika
2 tablespoons Pernod or Ricard
200 ml (7 fl oz) dry white wine
18 mussels, scrubbed and hairy beards removed
¼ teaspoon saffron threads
¼ teaspoon thyme leaves
6 baby octopus
16 raw prawns (shrimp), peeled and deveined, leaving the tails intact
500 g (1 lb 2 oz) swordfish steaks, cut into large chunks
400 g (14 oz) baby new potatoes
fennel greens, to garnish

serves 6

method Heat the oil in a large saucepan over medium heat. Add the fennel, leek and garlic. Stir in the paprika, season lightly and cook for 8 minutes, or until softened. Add the Pernod and wine, and stir for 1 minute, or until reduced by one-third.

Add the mussels, firstly discarding any open or cracked ones. Cover and cook for 1 minute, or until opened, discarding any that do not open. Remove from the pan to cool; remove from the shells and set aside.

Add the saffron and thyme to the pan, and cook for 1–2 minutes, stirring. Adjust the seasoning and transfer to a large, flameproof casserole dish.

Use a small sharp knife to remove the octopus heads. Grasp the bodies and push the beaks out with your index finger; remove and discard. Slit the heads and remove the gut. Mix the octopus, prawns, fish and potatoes into the stew. Cover and cook gently for 10 minutes, or until tender. Add the mussels, cover and heat through. Garnish with fennel greens and serve.

stuffed squid stew

100 ml (3½ fl oz) olive oil
1 large onion, finely chopped
2 garlic cloves, crushed
80 g (3 oz/1 cup) fresh breadcrumbs
1 egg, lightly beaten
60 g (2 oz) kefalotyri cheese, grated
60 g (2 oz) haloumi cheese, grated
4 large or 8 small squid (1 kg/2 lb 4 oz), cleaned
    (see Note)
1 small onion, finely chopped, extra
2 garlic cloves, crushed, extra
500 g (1 lb 2 oz) firm ripe tomatoes, peeled
    and diced
150 ml (5 fl oz) red wine
1 tablespoon chopped oregano
1 tablespoon chopped flat-leaf (Italian) parsley

serves 4

method Heat 2 tablespoons of the oil in a frying pan, add the onion and cook over medium heat for 3 minutes. Remove. Combine with the garlic, breadcrumbs, egg and cheeses. Season.

Pat the squid tubes dry with paper towels and, using a teaspoon, fill them three-quarters full with the stuffing. Do not pack them too tightly or the stuffing mixture will swell and burst out during cooking. Secure the ends with wooden toothpicks.

Heat the remaining oil in a large frying pan, add the squid and cook for 1–2 minutes on all sides. Remove. Add the extra onion and cook over medium heat for 3 minutes, or until soft, then add the extra garlic and cook for a further 1 minute. Stir in the tomato and wine, and simmer for 10 minutes, or until thick and pulpy, then stir in the oregano and parsley. Return the squid to the pan and cook, covered, for 20–25 minutes, or until tender. Serve warm with the tomato sauce or cool with a salad.

note *Ask the fishmonger to clean the squid. Or, discard the tentacles and cartilage. Rinse the tubes under running water and pull off the skin.*

spicy prawns

1 kg (2 lb 4 oz) raw prawns (shrimp), peeled
and deveined, leaving the tails intact
(reserve shells and heads)
1 teaspoon ground turmeric
60 ml (2 fl oz/¼ cup) oil
2 onions, finely chopped
4–6 garlic cloves, finely chopped
1–2 small green chillies, seeded and chopped
2 teaspoons ground cumin
2 teaspoons ground coriander
1 teaspoon paprika
90 g (3 oz/⅓ cup) plain yoghurt
80 ml (2½ fl oz/⅓ cup) thick (double/heavy)
cream
2 large handfuls coriander (cilantro) leaves,
chopped

serves 4–6

method   Bring 1 litre (35 fl oz/4 cups) water to the boil in a large saucepan. Add the reserved prawn shells and heads, reduce the heat and simmer for 25–30 minutes. Skim any scum that forms on the surface during cooking with a skimmer or slotted spoon. Drain, discard the shells and heads, and return the liquid to the pan. You will need 750 ml (26 fl oz/3 cups) liquid. Make up with water, if necessary. Add the turmeric and peeled prawns, and cook for 1 minute, or until the prawns just turn pink. Remove the prawns and set the stock aside.

Heat the oil in a large saucepan. Cook the onion on low–medium heat, stirring, for 8 minutes, or until light golden brown. Take care not to burn the onion. Add the garlic and chilli, cook for 2 minutes, then add the cumin, coriander and paprika, and cook, stirring, for 2–3 minutes, or until it becomes fragrant.

Gradually add the reserved prawn stock, bring to the boil and cook, stirring occasionally, for 35 minutes, or until the mixture has reduced by half and thickened.

Remove from the heat and stir in the yoghurt. Add the prawns and stir over low heat for 2–3 minutes, or until the prawns are warmed through, but do now allow the mixture to boil. Stir in the cream and coriander leaves. Cover and leave to stand for 15 minutes to allow the flavours to infuse. Reheat gently and serve with rice.

note   *You can also remove the prawn tails, if you prefer.*

whole fish casserole

1.25 kg (2 lb 12 oz) whole red bream or
   red snapper, cleaned
1 lemon
1 lemon, sliced, extra
60 ml (2 fl oz/¼ cup) olive oil
800 g (1 lb 12 oz) potatoes, thinly sliced
3 garlic cloves, thinly sliced
1 large handful finely chopped parsley
1 small red onion, thinly sliced
1 small dried chilli, seeded and finely chopped
1 red capsicum (pepper), cut into thin rings
1 green capsicum (pepper), cut into thin rings
2 bay leaves
3–4 thyme sprigs
60 ml (2 fl oz/¼ cup) dry sherry

serves 4–6

method Cut off and discard the fins from the fish and place it in a large non-metallic dish. Cut 2 thin slices from one end of the whole lemon and reserve. Squeeze the juice from the rest of the lemon inside the fish. Add 2 tablespoons of the oil. Refrigerate, covered, for 2 hours.

Preheat the oven to 190°C (375°F/Gas 5) and lightly oil a shallow earthenware baking dish large enough to hold the whole fish. Spread half the potato on the base and scatter the garlic, parsley, onion, chilli and capsicum on top. Season with salt and pepper. Cover with the rest of the potato. Pour in 80 ml (2½ fl oz/⅓ cup) water and sprinkle the remaining oil over the top. Cover the dish with foil and bake for 1 hour.

Increase the oven temperature to 220°C (425°F/Gas 7). Season the fish inside and out with salt and pepper, and place the bay leaves and thyme inside the cavity. Make three or four diagonal slashes on each side. Cut the reserved lemon slices in half and fit these into the slashes on one side of the fish, to resemble fins. Nestle the fish into the potatoes with extra lemon slices on top. Bake, uncovered, for 30 minutes, or until the fish is cooked through and the potato is golden and crusty.

Pour the dry sherry over the fish and return to the oven for 3 minutes. Serve straight from the dish.

100 EASY RECIPES ONE-POTS

coconut seafood and tofu curry

2 tablespoons soya bean oil, or cooking oil
500 g (1 lb 2 oz) firm white fish (ling, perch), cut
into 2 cm (¾ inch) cubes
250 g (9 oz) raw prawns (shrimp), peeled and
deveined, leaving the tails intact
2 x 400 ml (14 fl oz) tins coconut milk
1 tablespoon Thai red curry paste
4 fresh or 8 dried makrut (kaffir lime) leaves
2 tablespoons fish sauce
2 tablespoons finely chopped lemongrass
(white part only)
2 garlic cloves, crushed
1 tablespoon finely chopped fresh galangal
1 tablespoon shaved palm sugar (jaggery) or
soft brown sugar
300 g (10½ oz) silken firm tofu, cut into 1.5 cm
(⅝ inch) cubes
125 g (4½ oz/½ cup) bamboo shoots, trimmed
and cut into matchsticks
1 large red chilli, thinly sliced
2 teaspoons lime juice
spring onions (scallions), chopped, to garnish
coriander (cilantro) leaves, to garnish

serves 4

method Heat the oil in a large frying pan or wok over medium heat. Sear fish and prawns for 1 minute on each side. Remove the seafood from the pan.

Place 60 ml (2 fl oz/¼ cup) of the coconut milk and the curry paste in the frying pan, and cook over medium heat for 2 minutes, or until fragrant and the oil separates. Add the remaining coconut milk, makrut leaves, fish sauce, lemongrass, garlic, galangal, palm sugar and 1 teaspoon salt. Cook over low heat for 15 minutes.

Add the tofu, bamboo shoots and chilli. Simmer for a further 3–5 minutes. Return to medium heat, add the seafood and lime juice, and cook for a further 3 minutes, or until the seafood is just cooked. Serve with steamed rice and garnish with the spring onion and coriander.

chu chee seafood

2 x 270 ml (9½ fl oz) tins coconut cream
    (do not shake the tins)
55 g (2 oz/¼ cup) chu chee curry paste
500 g (1 lb 2 oz) scallops, roe removed
500 g (1 lb 2 oz) raw king prawns, peeled and
    deveined, leaving the tails intact
2–3 tablespoons fish sauce
2–3 tablespoons grated palm sugar (jaggery)
    or soft brown sugar
8 makrut (kaffir lime) leaves, finely shredded
2 red chillies, thinly sliced
2 large handfuls Thai basil leaves

serves 4

method Place 250 ml (9 fl oz/1 cup) of the thick coconut cream from the top of the tins in a wok. Heat until just boiling, then stir in the curry paste, reduce the heat and simmer for 10 minutes, or until fragrant and the oil just begins to separate.

Stir in the remaining coconut cream, the scallops and prawns, and cook for 5 minutes, or until tender. Add the fish sauce, palm sugar, makrut leaves and chilli, and cook for 1 minute. Stir in half of the basil and garnish with the remaining leaves before serving.

french-style octopus

1 kg (2 lb/4 oz) baby octopus
60 ml (2 fl oz/¼ cup) olive oil
1 large brown onion, chopped
2 garlic cloves
500 g (1 lb 2 oz) ripe tomatoes, peeled, seeded
and chopped
330 ml (11 fl oz/1⅓ cups) dry white wine
¼ teaspoon saffron threads
2 thyme sprigs
2 tablespoons roughly chopped flat-leaf
(Italian) parsley

serves 6

method To clean the octopus, use a small sharp knife and cut each head from the tentacles. Remove the eyes by cutting a round of flesh from the base of each head. To clean the heads, carefully slit them open and remove the gut, avoiding the ink sac. Rinse thoroughly. Cut the heads in half. Push out the beaks from the centre of the tentacles from the cut side. Cut the tentacles into sets of four or two, depending on the size of the octopus. Rinse under running water.

Blanch all the octopus in boiling water for 2 minutes, then drain and allow to cool slightly. Pat dry with paper towels.

Heat the olive oil in a heavy-based frying pan and cook the onion for 7–8 minutes over medium heat until lightly golden. Add the octopus and garlic to the pan, and cook for another 2–3 minutes. Add the tomato, wine, saffron and thyme. Add just enough water to cover the octopus.

Simmer, covered, for 1 hour. Uncover and cook for another 15 minutes, or until the octopus is tender and the sauce has thickened a little. The cooking time will vary depending upon the size of the octopus. Season to taste. Serve hot or at room temperature, sprinkled with parsley.

creamy garlic seafood stew

12 scallops, with roe
500 g (1 lb 2 oz) skinless firm white fish fillets
   (see Note)
6 raw Moreton Bay bugs/flat-head lobster
   or crabs
500 g (1 lb 2 oz) raw prawns (shrimp), peeled
   and deveined, leaving the tails intact
50 g (2 oz) butter
1 onion, finely chopped
5–6 large garlic cloves, finely chopped
125 ml (4 fl oz/½ cup) white wine
500 ml (17 fl oz/2 cups) cream
1½ tablespoons dijon mustard
2 teaspoons lemon juice
2 tablespoons chopped flat-leaf (Italian)
   parsley
lemon wedges, to serve

serves 6

method Slice or pull off any membrane or hard muscle from the scallops. Cut the fish into 2 cm (3/4 inch) cubes. Cut the heads off the bugs, then use kitchen scissors to cut down around the sides of the tail so you can flap open the shell. Remove the flesh in one piece, then slice each piece in half. Refrigerate all the seafood, covered, until ready to use.

Melt the butter in a frying pan and cook the onion and garlic over medium heat for 2 minutes, or until the onion is softened (be careful not to burn the garlic— it may become a little bitter).

Add the wine to the pan and cook for 4 minutes, or until reduced by half. Stir in the cream, mustard and lemon juice, and simmer for 5–6 minutes, or until reduced to almost half.

Add the prawns to the pan and cook for 1 minute, then add the bug meat and cook for another minute, or until white. Add the fish and cook for 2 minutes, or until cooked through (the flesh will flake easily when tested with a fork). Finally, add the scallops and cook for 1 minute. If any of the seafood is still not cooked, cook for another minute or so, but be careful not to overcook as this will result in tough flesh. Remove the frying pan from the heat and toss the parsley through. Season to taste. Serve with lemon wedges and bread, if desired.

note *Try using perch, ling, bream, tuna or blue-eye.*

balinese seafood curry

curry paste

2 tomatoes, peeled, seeded and roughly
chopped
5 small red chillies, seeded and chopped
5 garlic cloves, chopped
2 lemongrass stems (white part only), sliced
1 tablespoon coriander seeds, dry-roasted and
ground
1 teaspoon shrimp powder, dry-roasted
(see Note)
1 tablespoon ground almonds
¼ teaspoon ground nutmeg
1 teaspoon ground turmeric
60 g (2 oz/¼ cup) tamarind purée

1 tablespoon lime juice
250 g (9 oz) swordfish, cut into 3 cm
(1¼ inch) cubes
60 ml (2 fl oz/¼ cup) oil
2 red onions, chopped
2 small red chillies, seeded and sliced
400 g (14 oz) raw prawns (shrimp), peeled and
deveined, leaving the tails intact
250 g (9 oz) squid tubes, cut into 1 cm
(½ inch) rings
125 ml (4 fl oz/½ cup) fish stock
Thai basil leaves, shredded, to garnish

serves 6

method To make the curry paste, place all the ingredients in a blender or food processor, and blend to a thick paste.

Place the lime juice in a bowl and season with salt and freshly ground black pepper. Add the swordfish, toss to coat well and leave to marinate for 20 minutes.

Heat the oil in a saucepan or wok, add the onion, sliced red chilli and curry paste, and cook, stirring occasionally, over low heat for 10 minutes, or until fragrant.

Add the swordfish and prawns, and stir to coat in the curry paste mixture. Cook for 3 minutes, or until the prawns just turn pink, then add the squid and cook for 1 minute.

Add the stock and bring to the boil, then reduce the heat and simmer for 2 minutes, or until the seafood is cooked and tender. Season to taste with salt and freshly ground black pepper. Garnish with the shredded Thai basil leaves and serve.

note *If you cannot purchase shrimp powder, place some dried baby shrimp in a mortar and pestle and grind to a fine powder. Alternatively, you can place them in the small bowl of a food processor and process to a fine powder.*

jungle curry prawns

curry paste

10–12 dried red chillies
4 red Asian shallots (eschalots), chopped
4 garlic cloves, sliced
1 lemongrass stem (white part only), sliced
1 tablespoon finely chopped fresh galangal
2 small coriander (cilantro) roots, chopped
1 tablespoon finely chopped fresh ginger
1 tablespoon shrimp paste, dry-roasted
60 ml (2 fl oz/¼ cup) oil

1 tablespoon oil
1 garlic clove, crushed
40 g (1½ oz/¼ cup) ground candlenuts
1 tablespoon fish sauce
300 ml (10½ fl oz) fish stock
1 tablespoon whisky
600 g (1 lb 5 oz) raw prawns (shrimp), peeled
    and deveined, leaving the tails intact
1 small carrot, slivered
200 g (7 oz) snake (yard-long) beans, trimmed
    and cut into 2 cm (¾ inch) lengths
50 g (2 oz) bamboo shoots
3 makrut (kaffir lime) leaves, crushed
basil leaves, to garnish

serves 6

method To make the curry paste, soak the chillies in 250 ml (9 fl oz/1 cup) boiling water for about 10 minutes, then drain and place in a food processor with the remaining curry paste ingredients. Season with salt and white pepper, and process to a smooth paste.

Heat a wok over medium heat, add the oil and stir to coat the side. Add 3 tablespoons of the curry paste and the garlic, and cook, stirring constantly, for 5 minutes, or until fragrant. Stir in the candlenuts, fish sauce, stock, whisky, prawns, vegetables and makrut leaves, and bring to the boil. Reduce the heat and simmer for 5 minutes, or until cooked through. Garnish with the basil and serve with steamed rice.

100 EASY RECIPES ONE-POTS

goan fish curry

60 ml (2 fl oz/¼ cup) oil
1 large onion, finely chopped
4–5 garlic cloves, chopped
2 teaspoons grated fresh ginger
4–6 small dried red chillies
1 tablespoon coriander seeds
2 teaspoons cumin seeds
1 teaspoon ground turmeric
¼ teaspoon chilli powder
30 g (1 oz/⅓ cup) desiccated coconut
270 ml (9½ fl oz) coconut milk
2 tomatoes, peeled and chopped
2 tablespoons tamarind purée
1 tablespoon white vinegar
6 curry leaves
1 kg (2 lb 4 oz) boneless, skinless firm fish fillets,
such as flake or ling, cut into 8 cm
(3 inch) pieces
coriander (cilantro) leaves, to garnish

serves 6

method Heat the oil in a large saucepan. Add the onion and cook, stirring, over low heat for 10 minutes, or until softened. Add the garlic and ginger, and cook for a further 2 minutes.

Place the chillies, coriander seeds, cumin seeds, turmeric, chilli powder and coconut in a frying pan, and dry-fry (no oil), stirring constantly, over medium heat for 2 minutes, or until aromatic. Place in a food processor and finely grind.

Add the spice mixture, coconut milk, tomato, tamarind purée, vinegar and curry leaves to the onion mixture. Stir to mix thoroughly, add 250 ml (9 fl oz/1 cup) water and simmer for 10 minutes, or until mixture has softened and just thickened. Stir frequently to prevent sticking.

Add the fish and cook, covered, over low heat for 10 minutes, or until cooked through. Stir gently once or twice during cooking and add water if needed. Garnish with coriander and serve with rice and pappadums.

vegetarian

chickpea and herb dumpling soup

1 tablespoon oil
1 onion, chopped
2 garlic cloves, crushed
2 teaspoons ground cumin
1 teaspoon ground coriander
¼ teaspoon chilli powder
2 x 300 g (10½ oz) tins chickpeas, drained
875 ml (30 fl oz/3½ cups) vegetable stock
2 x 400 g (14 oz) tins chopped tomatoes
1 tablespoon chopped coriander (cilantro)
  leaves

dumplings

125 g (4½ oz/1 cup) self-raising flour
25 g (1 oz) butter, chopped
2 tablespoons grated parmesan cheese
2 tablespoons mixed chopped herbs (chives,
  flat-leaf (Italian) parsley and coriander
  (cilantro) leaves)
60 ml (2 fl oz/¼ cup) full-cream (whole) milk
crusty bread, to serve

serves 4

method Heat the oil in a large saucepan and cook the onion over medium heat for 2–3 minutes, or until soft. Add the garlic, cumin, ground coriander and chilli, and cook for 1 minute, or until fragrant. Add the chickpeas, stock and tomato. Bring to the boil, then reduce the heat and simmer, covered, for 10 minutes. Stir in the coriander leaves.

To make the dumplings, sift the flour into a bowl and add the chopped butter. Rub the butter into the flour with your fingertips until it resembles fine breadcrumbs. Stir in the parmesan and mixed fresh herbs. Make a well in the centre, add the milk and mix with a flat-bladed knife until just combined. Bring the dough together into a rough ball, divide into eight portions and roll into balls.

Add the dumplings to the soup, cover and simmer for 20 minutes, or until a skewer comes out clean when inserted into the centre of the dumplings. Serve with cracked black pepper and crusty bread.

100 EASY RECIPES ONE-POTS

spiced lentil soup

1 eggplant (aubergine)
60 ml (2 fl oz/¼ cup) olive oil
1 onion, finely chopped
2 teaspoons brown mustard seeds
2 teaspoons ground cumin
1 teaspoon garam masala
¼ teaspoon cayenne pepper (optional)
2 large carrots, cut into cubes
1 celery stalk, diced
400 g (14 oz) tin chopped tomatoes
100 g (3½ oz/1 cup) puy or small blue-green lentils
1 litre (35 fl oz/4 cups) vegetable stock
2 large handfuls coriander (cilantro) leaves, roughly chopped
125 g (4½ oz/½ cup) plain yoghurt

serves 4

method Cut the eggplant into cubes, place in a colander, sprinkle with salt and leave for 20 minutes. Rinse well and pat the eggplant dry with paper towels.

Heat the oil in a large saucepan over medium heat. Add the onion and cook for 5 minutes, or until softened. Add the eggplant, stir to coat in oil and cook for 3 minutes, or until softened.

Add the spices and the cayenne pepper (if using) and cook, stirring, for 1 minute, or until fragrant and the mustard seeds begin to pop. Add the carrot and celery and cook for 1 minute. Stir in the tomato, lentils and stock and bring to the boil. Reduce the heat and simmer for 40 minutes, or until the lentils are tender and the liquid is reduced to a thick stew-like soup. Season to taste with salt and freshly ground black pepper.

Stir the coriander into the soup just before serving. Ladle the soup into four warmed bowls and serve with a dollop of the yoghurt on top.

chunky vegetable soup

100 g (3½ oz/½ cup) dried red kidney beans or
   borlotti (cranberry) beans (see Note)
1 tablespoon olive oil
1 leek, halved lengthways, chopped
1 small onion, diced
2 carrots, chopped
2 celery stalks, chopped
1 large zucchini (courgette), chopped
1 tablespoon tomato paste (concentrated
   purée)
1 litre (35 fl oz/4 cups) vegetable stock
400 g (14 oz) pumpkin (winter squash), cut into
   2 cm (¾ inch) cubes
2 potatoes, cut into 2 cm (¾ inch) cubes
crusty wholemeal bread, to serve

serves 6

method Put the beans in a large bowl, cover with cold water and soak overnight. Rinse, then transfer to a saucepan, cover with cold water and cook on medium–high for 45 minutes, or until just tender. Drain and set aside.

Meanwhile, heat the oil in a large saucepan. Add the leek and onion, and cook over medium heat for 2–3 minutes without browning, or until they start to soften. Add the carrot, celery and zucchini, and cook for 3–4 minutes. Add the tomato paste and stir for a further 1 minute. Pour in the stock and 1.25 litres (44 fl oz/5 cups) water, and bring to the boil. Reduce the heat to low and simmer for 20 minutes.

Add the pumpkin, potato and beans, and simmer on low–medium heat for a further 20 minutes, or until the vegetables are tender and the beans are cooked. Season to taste. Serve immediately with crusty bread.

note *To save time, use a 400 g (14 oz) tin of red kidney beans instead of dried beans. Rinse well and leave out Step 1.*

100 EASY RECIPES ONE-POTS

mexican bean chowder

155 g (5½ oz/¾ cup) dried red kidney beans
165 g (6 oz/¾ cup) dried Mexican black beans (see Note)
1 tablespoon oil
1 onion, chopped
2 garlic cloves, crushed
½–1 teaspoon chilli powder
1 tablespoon ground cumin
2 teaspoons ground coriander
2 x 400 g (14 oz) tins chopped tomatoes
750 ml (26 fl oz/3 cups) vegetable stock
1 red capsicum (pepper), chopped
1 green capsicum (pepper), chopped
440 g (15½ oz) tin corn kernels
2 tablespoons tomato paste (concentrated purée)
grated cheddar cheese, to serve
sour cream, to serve

serves 6

method Soak the kidney beans and black beans in separate bowls in plenty of cold water overnight. Drain. Place in a large saucepan, cover with water and bring to the boil. Reduce the heat and simmer for 45 minutes, or until tender. Drain.

Heat the oil in a large saucepan, add the onion and cook over medium heat until soft. Add the garlic, chilli powder, cumin and coriander, and cook for 1 minute. Stir in the tomato, stock, capsicum, corn and tomato paste. Cook, covered, for 25–30 minutes. Add the beans during the last 10 minutes of cooking. Stir occasionally. Serve topped with the grated cheddar and a spoonful of sour cream.

note *Mexican black beans are also known as black turtle beans.*

barley soup with golden parsnips

200 g (7 oz) pearl barley
1 tablespoon oil
2 onions, chopped
2 garlic cloves, finely chopped
2 carrots, chopped
2 potatoes, chopped
2 celery stalks, chopped
2 bay leaves, torn in half
2 litres (70 fl oz/8 cups) vegetable stock
125 ml (4 fl oz/½ cup) full-cream (whole) milk
40 g (1½ oz) butter
3 parsnips, cubed
1 teaspoon soft brown sugar
chopped flat-leaf (Italian) parsley, to serve

serves 6

method Soak the barley in water overnight. Drain. Place in a saucepan with 2 litres (70 fl oz/8 cups) water. Bring to the boil, then reduce the heat and simmer, partially covered, for 1¼ hours, or until tender. Drain the barley.

Heat the oil in a large saucepan, add the onion, garlic, carrot, potato and celery, and cook for 3 minutes. Stir well and cook, covered, for 15 minutes over low heat, stirring occasionally.

Add the barley, bay leaves, stock, milk, 2 teaspoons of salt and 1 teaspoon of pepper. Bring to the boil, then reduce the heat and simmer the soup, partially covered, for around 35 minutes. If the soup is too thick, add about 250 ml (9 fl oz/1 cup) cold water, a little at a time, until it reaches your preferred consistency.

While the soup is simmering, melt the butter in a frying pan, add the parsnip and toss in the butter. Sprinkle with the sugar and cook until golden brown and tender. Serve the parsnip on top of the soup and sprinkle with the parsley and, if desired, season with cracked black pepper.

100 EASY RECIPES ONE-POTS

creamy potato casserole

750 g (1 lb 10 oz) all-purpose potatoes (see Note)
1 onion
125 g (4½ oz/1 cup) grated cheddar cheese
375 ml (13 fl oz/1½ cups) cream
2 teaspoons vegetable stock powder

serves 4–6

method Preheat the oven to 180°C (350°F/Gas 4). Peel the potatoes and thinly slice them. Peel the onion and slice it into rings.

Arrange a layer of overlapping potato slices in the base of a large casserole dish. Top the potato slices with a layer of the onion rings. Divide the grated cheese in half and set aside one half to use as a topping. Sprinkle a little of the remaining grated cheese over the onion rings. Continue layering in this order until all the potato and the onion have been used, finishing with a little of the grated cheese.

Pour the cream into a small jug, add the vegetable stock powder and whisk gently until the mixture is thoroughly combined. Carefully pour the cream mixture over the layered potato and onion slices, and sprinkle the top with the reserved grated cheese. Bake the casserole, uncovered, for 40 minutes, or until the potato is tender, the cheese has melted and the top is golden brown.

note *Waxy or all-purpose potatoes are best to use in this recipe because they hold their shape better when slow-cooked. If you have a mandolin, use it to cut the potatoes into very thin slices. If not, make sure you use a very sharp knife.*

vegetable tagine

2 tablespoons oil
2 onions, chopped
1 teaspoon ground ginger
2 teaspoons ground paprika
2 teaspoons ground cumin
1 cinnamon stick
pinch saffron threads
1.5 kg (3 lb 5 oz) vegetables, peeled and cut into large chunks, such as carrot, eggplant (aubergine), orange sweet potato, parsnip, potato, pumpkin (winter squash)
½ preserved lemon, rinsed, pith and flesh removed, thinly sliced
400 g (14 oz) tin chopped tomatoes
250 ml (9 fl oz/1 cup) vegetable stock
100 g (3½ oz) dried pears, halved
50 g (2 oz) pitted prunes
2 zucchini (courgettes), cut into large chunks
300 g (10½ oz) couscous
1 tablespoon olive oil
2 tablespoons chopped flat-leaf (Italian) parsley
50 g (2 oz/⅓ cup) blanched almonds

serves 4–6

method Preheat the oven to 180°C (350°F/Gas 4). Heat the oil in a large flameproof dish, add the onion and cook over medium heat for 5 minutes. Add the spices and cook for 3 minutes.

Add the chopped mixed vegetables and cook, stirring, until coated and the vegetables soften. Add the lemon, tomato, stock, pears and prunes. Cover with a lid, transfer to the oven and cook for 30 minutes. Add the zucchini and cook for 15–20 minutes, or until the vegetables are tender.

Cover the couscous with the olive oil and 500 ml (17 fl oz/2 cups) boiling water, and stand until all the water absorbs. Fluff with a fork.

Remove the cinnamon stick from the vegetables, then stir in the parsley. Serve on a large platter with the couscous on the bottom and the vegetables on top. Sprinkle with almonds.

100 EASY RECIPES ONE-POTS

bean and capsicum stew

200 g (7 oz/1 cup) dried haricot beans
(see Note)
2 tablespoons olive oil
2 large garlic cloves, crushed
1 red onion, halved and cut into thin wedges
1 red capsicum (pepper), cut into 1.5 cm
($^5/_8$ inch) squares
1 green capsicum (pepper), cut into 1.5 cm
($^5/_8$ inch) squares
2 x 400 g (14 oz) tins chopped tomatoes
2 tablespoons tomato paste (concentrated
purée)
500 ml (17 fl oz/2 cups) vegetable stock
2 tablespoons chopped basil
125 g (4½ oz/⅔ cup) Kalamata olives, pitted
1–2 teaspoons soft brown sugar
basil leaves, to garnish

serves 4–6

method Put the beans in a large bowl, cover with cold water and soak overnight. Rinse well, then transfer to a saucepan, cover with cold water and cook for 45 minutes, or until just tender. Drain.

Heat the oil in a large saucepan. Cook the garlic and onion wedges over medium heat for 2–3 minutes, or until the onion is soft. Add the red and green capsicum, and cook for a further 5 minutes.

Stir in the tomato, tomato paste, stock and beans. Simmer, covered, for 40 minutes, or until the beans are cooked through. Stir in the basil, olives and sugar. Season with salt and pepper, garnish with basil leaves. Serve piping hot with crusty bread.

note 200 g (1 cup) of dried haricot beans yields about 2½ cups cooked beans. You can use 2½ cups tinned haricot or borlotti (cranberry) beans if you prefer.

green tofu curry

method To make the curry paste, place all the ingredients in a food processor and process until it is smooth.

Heat the oil in a frying pan, add the onion and cook for 5 minutes, or until soft. Add 4 tablespoons curry paste (or more for a stronger flavour) and cook, stirring, for 2 minutes. Stir in the coconut cream and 250 ml (9 fl oz/1 cup) water, and season with salt. Bring to the boil and add the makrut leaves and tofu. Reduce the heat and simmer for 8 minutes, stirring often. Stir in the lime juice and shredded Thai basil, and serve.

hint *The recipe for the curry paste makes 1 cup, but you will only need ⅓ cup. Freeze the remaining paste in two portions to use at a later date.*

yellow vegetable curry

60 ml (2 fl oz/¼ cup) oil
1 onion, finely chopped
2 tablespoons Thai yellow curry paste
250 g (9 oz) potato, diced
200 g (7 oz) zucchini (courgettes), diced
150 g (5½ oz) red capsicum (pepper), diced
100 g (3½ oz) green beans, trimmed
50 g (2 oz) bamboo shoots, trimmed
and sliced
250 ml (9 fl oz/1 cup) vegetable stock
400 ml (14 fl oz) tin coconut cream
Thai basil leaves, to garnish

serves 6

method Heat the oil in a large saucepan, add the onion and cook over medium heat for about 5 minutes, or until softened. Add the curry paste and cook, stirring, for 2 minutes, or until fragrant.

Add all the vegetables and cook, stirring, over high heat for 2 minutes. Pour in the stock, reduce the heat to medium and cook, covered, for 15–20 minutes, or until the vegetables are tender. Cook, uncovered, over high heat for 5–10 minutes, or until the sauce has reduced slightly.

Stir in the coconut cream, and season with salt. Bring to the boil, stirring frequently, then reduce the heat and simmer for 5 minutes. Garnish with the Thai basil leaves.

spicy vegetable stew with dhal

dhal

165 g (6 oz/¾ cup) yellow split peas
5 cm (2 inch) piece fresh ginger, grated
2–3 garlic cloves, crushed
1 red chilli, seeded and chopped

2 tablespoons oil
1 teaspoon yellow mustard seeds
1 teaspoon cumin seeds
1 teaspoon ground cumin
½ teaspoon garam masala
1 red onion, cut into thin wedges
3 tomatoes, peeled, seeded and chopped
3 slender eggplants (aubergines), cut into 2 cm
    (¾ inch) slices
2 carrots, cut into 2 cm (¾ inch) slices
¼ cauliflower, cut into florets
375 ml (13 fl oz/1½ cups) vegetable stock
2 small zucchini (courgettes), cut into 3 cm
    (1¼ inch) slices
80 g (3 oz/½ cup) frozen peas
1 large handful coriander (cilantro) leaves,
    plus extra, to garnish.

serves 4–6

method Put the split peas in a bowl, cover with water and soak for 2 hours. Drain. To make the dhal put the split peas in a large saucepan with the ginger, garlic, chilli and 750 ml (26 fl oz/3 cups) water. Bring to the boil, reduce the heat and simmer for 45 minutes, or until soft.

Heat the oil in a large saucepan. Cook the spices over medium heat for 30 seconds, or until fragrant. Add the onion and cook for a further 2 minutes, or until the onion is soft. Stir in the tomato, eggplant, carrot and cauliflower.

Add the dhal mixture and stock, mix together well and simmer, covered, for 45 minutes, or until the vegetables are tender. Stir occasionally. Add the zucchini and peas during the last 10 minutes of cooking. Stir in the coriander leaves, then garnish and serve.

100 EASY RECIPES ONE-POTS

indonesian vegetable and coconut curry

5 candlenuts or macadamia nuts
75 g (2½ oz) red Asian shallots (eschalots)
2 garlic cloves
2 teaspoons sambal oelek (South-East Asian chilli paste)
¼ teaspoon ground turmeric
1 teaspoon grated fresh galangal
1 tablespoon peanut butter

2 tablespoons oil
1 onion, sliced
400 ml (14 fl oz) tin coconut cream
200 g (7 oz) carrots, cut into matchsticks
200 g (7 oz) snake (yard-long) beans, trimmed, cut into 7 cm (2¾ inch) lengths
300 g (10½ oz) Chinese cabbage, roughly shredded
100 g (3½ oz) fresh shiitake mushrooms
¼ teaspoon sugar

serves 6

method To make the curry paste, place the candlenuts, shallots, garlic, sambal oelek, turmeric, galangal and peanut butter in a food processor, and process to a smooth paste.

Heat the oil in a large saucepan over low heat. Cook the curry paste, stirring, for 5 minutes, or until fragrant. Add the onion and cook for 5 minutes. Stir in 60 ml (2 fl oz/¼ cup) coconut cream and cook, stirring constantly, for 2 minutes, or until thickened. Add the carrot and beans, and cook over high heat for 3 minutes. Stir in the cabbage, mushrooms and 250 ml (9 fl oz/1 cup) water. Cook over high heat for 8–10 minutes, or until the vegetables are nearly cooked.

Stir in the remaining coconut cream and the sugar, and season with salt. Bring to the boil, stirring constantly, then reduce the heat and simmer for 8–10 minutes, to allow the flavours to develop.

potato curry

curry paste

4 cardamom pods
1 teaspoon grated fresh ginger
2 garlic cloves
6 small red chillies
1 teaspoon cumin seeds
40 g (1 ½ oz/¼ cup) raw cashew nut pieces
1 tablespoon white poppy seeds (khus)
   (see Note)
1 cinnamon stick
6 cloves

1 kg (2 lb 4 oz) potatoes, cubed
2 onions, roughly chopped
2 tablespoons oil
½ teaspoon ground turmeric
1 teaspoon besan (chickpea flour)
250 g (9 oz/1 cup) plain yoghurt
coriander (cilantro) leaves, to garnish

serves 6

method To make the curry paste, lightly crush the cardamom pods with the flat side of a heavy knife. Remove the seeds, discarding the pods. Place the seeds and the remaining curry paste ingredients in a food processor, and process to a smooth paste.

Bring a large saucepan of lightly salted water to the boil. Add the potato and cook for 5–6 minutes, or until just tender. Drain.

Place the onion in a food processor and process in short bursts until it is finely ground but not puréed. Heat the oil in a large saucepan, add the ground onion and cook over low heat for 5 minutes. Add the curry paste and cook, stirring, for a further 5 minutes, or until fragrant. Stir in the potato, turmeric, salt to taste and 250 ml (9 fl oz/1 cup) water.

Reduce the heat and simmer, tightly covered, for 10 minutes, or until the potato is cooked but not breaking up and the sauce has thickened slightly.

Combine the besan with the yoghurt, add to the potato mixture and cook, stirring, over low heat for 5 minutes, or until thickened again. Garnish with the coriander leaves.

note *White poppy seeds (khus) should not be mistaken for black and do not yield opium. They are off-white, odourless and flavourless until roasted when they have a slight sesame aroma and flavour. If they are not available, replace the poppy seeds with sesame seeds.*

100 EASY RECIPES ONE-POTS

ratatouille

100 ml (3½ fl oz) olive oil
500 g (1 lb 2 oz) eggplants (aubergines), cut into 2 cm (¾ inch) cubes
375 g (13 oz) zucchini (courgettes), cut into 2 cm (¾ inch) slices
1 green capsicum (pepper), seeded, cut into 2 cm (¾ inch) cubes
1 red onion, cut into 2 cm (¾ inch) wedges
3 garlic cloves, finely chopped
¼ teaspoon cayenne pepper
2 teaspoons chopped thyme
2 bay leaves
6 vine-ripened tomatoes, peeled and roughly chopped
1 tablespoon red wine vinegar
1 teaspoon caster (superfine) sugar
4 tablespoons shredded basil

serves 4–6

method Heat 2 tablespoons of the oil in a large saucepan and cook the eggplant over medium heat for 4–5 minutes, or until soft but not browned. Remove all the eggplant from the pan.

Add another 2 tablespoons oil to the pan and cook the zucchini slices for 3–4 minutes, or until softened. Remove the zucchini from the pan. Add the capsicum to the pan, cook for 2 minutes, then remove.

Heat the remaining oil in the pan, add the onion wedges and cook for 2–3 minutes, or until softened. Add the garlic, cayenne pepper, thyme and bay leaves, and cook, stirring, for 1 minute. Return the cooked eggplant, zucchini and capsicum to the pan, and add the tomato, vinegar and sugar. Simmer for 20 minutes, stirring occasionally. Stir in the basil and season with salt and black pepper. You can serve ratatouille hot or cold.

note *Ratatouille takes quite a long time to prepare and so is traditionally made in large quantities. It is then eaten over several days as an hors d'oeuvre, side dish or main meal.*

chu chee tofu

method To make the curry paste, place all the ingredients in a food processor or spice grinder and process until smooth.

Heat the oil in a large saucepan, add the onion and cook over medium heat for 4–5 minutes, or until it starts to brown. Add 3 tablespoons of the curry paste and cook, stirring, for 2 minutes.

Stir in the coconut milk and 125 ml (4 fl oz/½ cup) water, and season with salt. Bring slowly to the boil, stirring constantly. Add the tofu puffs, then reduce the heat and simmer, stirring frequently, for 5 minutes, or until the sauce thickens slightly. Garnish with the coriander sprigs.

100 EASY RECIPES ONE-POTS

vegetarian chilli

130 g (4½ oz/¾ cup) burghul (bulgur)
2 tablespoons olive oil
1 large onion, finely chopped
2 garlic cloves, crushed
1 teaspoon chilli powder
2 teaspoons ground cumin
1 teaspoon cayenne pepper
½ teaspoon ground cinnamon
2 x 400 g (14 oz) tins chopped tomatoes
750 ml (26 fl oz/3 cups) vegetable stock
440 g (15½ oz) tin red kidney beans, drained
and rinsed
2 x 300 g (10½ oz) tins chickpeas, drained
and rinsed
310 g (11 oz) tin corn kernels, drained
2 tablespoons tomato paste (concentrated
purée)
corn chips and sour cream, to serve

serves 6–8

method Soak the burghul in 250 ml (9 fl oz/1 cup) hot water for 10 minutes. Heat the oil in a large heavy-based saucepan and cook the onion for 10 minutes, stirring often, until soft and golden.

Add the garlic, chilli, cumin, cayenne and cinnamon, and cook, stirring, for 1 minute.

Add the tomato, stock and burghul. Bring to the boil and simmer for 10 minutes. Stir in the beans, chickpeas, corn and tomato paste, and simmer for 20 minutes, stirring often. Serve with corn chips and sour cream.

cheese and pea curry

paneer

2 litres (70 fl oz/8 cups) full-cream (whole) milk
80 ml (2½ fl oz/⅓ cup) lemon juice

curry paste

2 large onions, chopped
3 garlic cloves
1 teaspoon grated fresh ginger
1 teaspoon cumin seeds
3 dried red chillies
1 teaspoon cardamom seeds
4 cloves
1 teaspoon fennel seeds
2 pieces cassia bark

oil, for deep-frying
500 g (1 lb 2 oz) frozen peas
2 tablespoons oil
400 g (14 oz) tomato paste (concentrated
    purée)
1 tablespoon garam masala
1 teaspoon ground coriander
¼ teaspoon ground turmeric
1 tablespoon cream
coriander (cilantro) leaves, to garnish

serves 6

method To make the paneer, place the milk in a large saucepan, bring to the boil, stir in the lemon juice and turn off the heat. Stir the mixture for 1–2 seconds as it curdles. Place in a colander and leave for 30 minutes for the whey to drain off. Place the paneer curds on a clean, flat surface, cover with a plate, weigh down and leave for at least 4 hours.

To make the curry paste, place all the ingredients in a spice grinder or food processor, and grind to a smooth paste.

Cut the solid paneer into 2 cm (³⁄₄ inch) cubes. Fill a deep heavy-based saucepan one-third full of oil and heat to 180°C (350°F), or until a cube of bread browns in 15 seconds. Cook the paneer in batches for 2–3 minutes, or until golden. Drain on paper towels.

Cook the peas in a saucepan of boiling water for 3 minutes, or until tender. Drain.

Heat the oil in a large saucepan, add the curry paste and cook over medium heat for 4 minutes, or until fragrant. Add the tomato paste, spices, cream and 125 ml (4 fl oz/¹⁄₂ cup) water. Season with salt, and simmer over medium heat for 5 minutes. Add the paneer and peas, and cook for 3 minutes. Garnish with coriander leaves, and serve hot.

autumn vegetable stew

185 g (6 oz) frozen broad (fava) beans, thawed
(see Notes)
150 g (5½ oz) baby onions (see Notes)
50 g (1¾ oz) butter
2 teaspoons olive oil
400 g (14 oz) small parsnips
150 g (5½ oz) Jerusalem artichokes
2 tablespoons plain (all-purpose) flour
580 ml (20¼ fl oz/3 cups) vegetable stock
300 ml (10½ fl oz) cream
2 teaspoons grated lemon zest
1 teaspoon grated orange zest
400 g (14 oz) baby carrots, trimmed
500 g (1 lb 2 oz) baby turnips, trimmed

serves 4–6

method Peel and discard the tough outer skin of the broad beans. Carefully peel the onions, leaving the flat root end attached, then cut a cross through the root end of each onion.

Heat the butter and oil in a large heavy-based saucepan until foamy. Add the onions and cook for 7 minutes over low–medium heat, turning often to colour evenly.

While the onions are browning, peel the parsnips and artichokes, and cut them into bite-sized pieces. Add to the saucepan and toss well. Scatter the flour over the onion, parsnip and artichokes, toss to coat and cook for 2 minutes.

Stir in the chicken stock, cream, lemon zest and orange zest. Bring to the boil, stirring, then reduce the heat and simmer for 7 minutes, or until the vegetables are half-cooked.

Add the carrots and turnips, and toss well. Cover the pan and cook for 4–5 minutes, or until the vegetables are just tender. Season well with salt and freshly ground black pepper, stir in the peeled broad beans to heat through, and serve.

notes *Fresh broad beans can be used. Add them with the carrots and turnips. Baby vegetables have a sweet, delicate flavour. If unavailable, choose the smallest vegetables and cook them for a few minutes longer.*

Published in 2010 by Bay Books,
an imprint of Murdoch Books Pty Limited.

Murdoch Books Australia
Pier 8/9,
23 Hickson Road,
Millers Point NSW 2000
Phone: +61 (0)2 8220 2000
Fax: +61 (0)2 8220 2558
www.murdochbooks.com.au

Murdoch Books UK Limited
Erico House,
6th Floor North, 93–99 Upper Richmond Road,
Putney, London SW15 2TG
Phone: + 44 (0) 20 8785 5995
Fax: + 44 (0) 20 8785 5985
www.murdochbooks.co.uk

Chief Executive: Juliet Rogers

Publisher: Lynn Lewis
Senior Designer: Heather Menzies
Designer: Transformer Design
Editor: Zoë Harpham
Editorial Coordinator: Liz Malcolm
Index: Jo Rudd
Production: Alexandra Gonzalez

National Library of Australia Cataloguing-in-Publication Data:
Title: One-pots
ISBN: 978-1-74266-008-0 (pbk)
Series: 100 Easy Recipes
Notes: Includes index
Subjects: One-dish meals. Cooking.
Dewey Number: 641.82

Printed by C & C Offset Printing Co. Ltd. PRINTED IN CHINA.